Creating a Circle of Collaborative Spiritual Leadership

Creating a Circle of Collaborative Spiritual Leadership

Roberto Trostli, editor

Pedagogical Section Council of North America

Printed by:
Waldorf Publications at the
Research Institute for Waldorf Education
38 Main Street
Chatham, NY 12037

Title: *Creating a Circle of Collaborative Spiritual Leadership*
Editor: Roberto Trostli
Layout: Ann Erwin
Proofreading: Tertia Gale, Ann Erwin
Cover print: "Elemental Art," one in a series of three illuminating a
haiku, 10"x10" oil on canvas, by kind permission of the artist, Ursula
Stone www.ursulastone.com, and the owner, Xavier Curry.

ISBN: 978-1-936367-48-1

This is a selection of articles previously printed in
The Research Bulletin, Volumes 16 and 17, 2011–2012,
published by the Research Institute for Waldorf Education,
ed. Elan Leibner, PO Box 307, Wilton, NH 03086.

Contents

Introduction

Roberto Trostli

This book is the culmination of a three-year project of the Pedagogical Section Council of the School for Spiritual Science of the Anthroposophical Society in North America. Founded in 1982, the Council seeks to strengthen the foundational spiritual impulses of Waldorf education; one of its tasks is to publish texts that help teachers and schools deepen their work.

I was a member of the Pedagogical Section Council for ten years, and in every one of those meetings the topic of the college of teachers came up, either in reports about schools, or while discussing another subject, or, increasingly, as our major focus. At times we all seemed to be in agreement about what a college should be; at other times our differences stood out. What was always clear to us, though, was that we needed to understand the college better if Waldorf schools were to grow stronger and Waldorf education to fulfill its mission.

This book weaves together the threads of our many conversations. In each article you will read the author's words, but what gives them resonance are the many contributions from colleagues who put into words what needed to be said. In the *Teachers' Imagination* Rudolf Steiner describes how the archangels work with us, carrying from one to the other what each has to give to the other. From that activity, a chalice is created, and into that chalice can fall a drop of the light of wisdom. This book is the result of such a chalice. As you read it, we hope that you will be able to listen through the words to the strivings of the authors and to the counsel of their peers and of the beings who inspired and guided them. The wisdom to be found in this chalice arose from a true collaboration, the kind of collaboration that occurs in a college of teachers.

As a collection of articles exploring aspects of the college of teachers, this book is not meant to be comprehensive but rather to provide a starting point for colleagues and colleges to work together to try to understand the mysteries of this human-spiritual community at the center of our schools. We hope that this collection will stimulate further discussion and research, for there is still so much to discover about this community that stands at the center of the Waldorf school.

What does this book contain? In the first article, "On Earth as It Is in Heaven," I examine the founding of the first college of teachers as a mystery that can reveal Rudolf Steiner's intentions for how Waldorf schools can help spirit and matter find their proper relationship to one another. In our Pedagogical Section Council meetings, I often wrestled with the challenge of bridging big ideas and little details. This article captures some of those struggles, leaving us more with questions than answers.

In "Spirit Is Never without Matter; Matter Never without Spirit," Liz Beaven shares the history of the college of teachers at the Sacramento Waldorf School. She describes the college's founding and how—over the years—it struggled to find effective forms that could fulfill its spiritual and earthly mandates. Liz's description of the stages the college went through and the different ways in which it worked remind us that a school is an organism in a process of continual change. If a college is to serve this organism, it too must change.

During my tenure on the Pedagogical Section Council, there was hardly a meeting when Jane Wulsin didn't speak about the central importance of *Teachers' Imagination* to our work as teachers and as college members. Every time she spoke about it, I was struck anew by the rightness and importance of what she was saying. In "An Essential Teacher Meditation" Jane shares the essence of what she brought to us from year to year. Readers will recognize how decades of working with this meditation resound through Jane's carefully chosen words.

Every member of a group enhances the group's work through his or her unique gifts and capacities. When Holly Koteen-Soulé joined the Pedagogical Section Council, our meetings became more thoughtful, gracious, and harmonious. In "Creating Space for Spirit," readers can sense some of what Holly has brought to our Council meetings. In this article she explores how we can create meetings in which we can learn the social art and truly meet one another.

In 1998 Elan Leibner came to a Council meeting to share his experiences and ideas about working meditatively as a group. He led us in a contemplative exercise, the results of which resonated through the rest of our weekend. Once he joined the Council, he helped us deepen our work through group meditative practices. In "Contemplative Work in the College Meeting," Elan describes how we can work together meditatively in a disciplined and artistic manner to get beyond our narrow, earthly selves.

Over the years, Betty Staley has continually impressed her Pedagogical Section Council colleagues with her interest, her enthusiasm, and, most of all, her capacity for work. At every meeting we would hear about what Betty was working on: research, a project, a book—all in addition to a full load of teaching, consulting, and lecturing. "The Three Castles" is an example of Betty at her best: a teacher in such command of her subject and a spiritual researcher of such maturity that she is able to find the inner connections between the mysteries contained in a work such as *Parzival* and the mysteries of individual and collegial work.

When we embarked on this project, the Council was concerned that a collection like this might be perceived as being too authoritative. Now that this volume is complete, the concerns seems unfounded. The authors' earnestness shines through their words. They speak with modesty and restraint, offering ideas with conviction but with the recognition that these ideas are far larger than these modest expressions. Rudolf Steiner tells us that every idea that becomes an ideal creates forces in our souls. We hope that the ideas in this collection will stimulate teachers and colleges to contemplate, discuss, and work together to discover how to transform such ideas into ideals.

Members of the Pedagogical Section Council

Henry Barnes (F) †
Hans Gebert (F) †
Werner Glas (F) †
Magda Lissau (F) †
René Querido (F) †
Ekkehard Piening (F) †
James Pewtherer (F) *
Virginia Sease (F)
Patricia Livingston (F)
Anne Charles †
*Betty Staley**
Jane Wulsin*
Joan Almon

Antje Ghaznavi*
*Ina Jaehnig**
Astrid Schmitt-Stegmann
*Frances Vig**
Roberto Trostli*
Susan Howard
*Douglas Gerwin**
*Elan Leibner**
*Judy Lucas**
*Holly Koteen-Soulé**
Tari Steinrueck
Jennifer Snyder
Laura Radefeld

(F)   Founding members of the Council
†   Members of the Council who have crossed the threshold
*   Members of the Council who participated in the discussions that led to this publication
italics Current members of the Council

On Earth as It Is in Heaven

The Tasks of the College of Teachers
in the Light of the Founding Impulse of Waldorf Education

Roberto Trostli

Introduction

At the center of the Waldorf school stands the College of Teachers.[1] What is the College? What are its tasks? Who serves on the College? Why is it important for a Waldorf school to have a College? The answers to these questions will help us understand the mission and tasks of the Waldorf school.

In this work, I will address these fundamental questions about the College in light of the founding of the first Waldorf school in 1919. I will also share some ideas about the College that I have developed in nearly three decades of working with Colleges. I hope that my work will inspire others to delve deeply into these questions and to develop their own perspectives.

I. What Is the College of Teachers and What Are Its Tasks?

A Waldorf school is more than just another independent school that provides a developmental education. It is an organization that seeks to allow the spiritual impulses of our time to manifest on earth in order to transform society. The group that is primarily responsible for recognizing and realizing this mission is the College of Teachers. The College does so by working in two realms: the material and the spiritual. This essential feature was revealed during the preparatory course for the founding of the first Waldorf school in Stuttgart, Germany. By examining what Rudolf Steiner presented in *The Opening Address* and *The College Founding*, we will begin to sense how the College can bridge and balance the worlds of matter and spirit. (These texts are included in the Appendix.)

The Opening Address and The College Founding

The Opening Address was given by Rudolf Steiner on the evening of August 20, 1919, prior to the preparatory course for the teachers of the first Waldorf school. In The Opening Address, Rudolf Steiner identified two major goals for the school:

    (1) to achieve a renewal of modern spiritual life by reforming and revolutionizing the educational system, and

    (2) to demonstrate the effectiveness of anthroposophy through a new art of education.

The Opening Address also described how teachers could work towards these goals individually and collectively in a "teachers' republic."

The College Founding was given the following morning as the opening to the first lecture in the series now known as the *Study of Man*.[2] There Rudolf Steiner spoke again about the goals of the Waldorf school and the tasks of the teachers, highlighting the cosmic importance of the school's founding. At the center of The College Founding, Rudolf Steiner presented the College Imagination, which shows the teachers how to work with the beings of the Third Hierarchy: the Angels, the Archangels, and the Archai.

With these two addresses Rudolf Steiner established the College as the place in the school where teachers work on earthly and spiritual tasks. The Opening Address deals with the earthly aspects. These include the societal context, the need to make anthroposophy practical, the compromises that will be needed, and the school's administration. The College Founding deals with the spiritual aspects. These include the cosmic context, our relationship to one another, and how we can work with spiritual beings.

In these addresses Rudolf Steiner presented the teachers with two sides of their work together. The Opening Address poses a set of earthly questions and challenges, and The College Founding provides a way of looking at these from a spiritual perspective. Here are some examples:

The Opening Address: How will we renew spiritual life by reforming and revolutionizing the educational system?
The College Founding: We will see our work not as simply a matter of intellect or feeling, but, in the highest sense, as a moral, spiritual task.

The Opening Address: How will The Waldorf School serve as living proof of the effectiveness of the anthroposophical orientation toward life?
The College Founding: We will create, from the very beginning, a connection between our activity and the spiritual worlds.

The Opening Address: How will we deal with the state's goals and standards and make the necessary compromises?
The College Founding: We will not view the founding of this school as an everyday occurrence, but as a ceremony held within the Cosmic Order.

Both of these addresses have a similar structure; each is like a triptych. The beginning and ending sections of each address mirror each other, describing the context, the tasks, and the qualities that will be needed to perform these tasks. These outer sections frame the most important question for the College: How can these important tasks be performed? Like a triptych, whose middle section carries the central image, the middle sections of the two addresses show how teachers can work together on the earthly and spiritual planes. From the chart below we can see that The College Founding considers the points in The Opening Address from a spiritual perspective.

From The Opening Address:
1. Each teacher needs to work in full responsibility.
2. We will work together in a "teachers' republic."
3. We will develop a spirit of unity by our work with the preparatory course.

From The College Founding:
1. Our Angel gives us strength for our individual work.
2. The Archangels give us courage for our collective work.
3. The Archai give us light; we work with the Spirit of the Times.

At the very beginning of the founding of The Waldorf School, Rudolf Steiner already established the task of the College: to bridge and balance the earthly and spiritual realities in the service of the school and the education of the students.

Finding the Balance
A College of Teachers has earthly tasks and spiritual tasks, and the College in each school must find the proper balance between them. This balance will change as the school's

circumstances change. It may even change during the course of the school year. At every meeting, the College must find the balance between its earthly focus—administration, personnel, facilities, finances, and so forth—and its spiritual focus—anthroposophy, child development, the curriculum, methodology, and so forth. Whether a College focuses more on earthly matters or spiritual matters depends on the needs of the school. What is most important is that earthly matters be informed from the point of view of the spirit and that spiritual matters be informed by down-to-earth practicality.

The word "balance" comes from the Latin name for scale. It is derived from the words *bi* and *lanx*, which together mean "two dishes" or "trays." The trays of a scale hold what is to be weighed. Unequal weights cause the dishes to move vertically, with the heavier dish ending up lower than the lighter. Equal weights result in the trays' reaching the horizontal, the balance point.

The scale also has a bar that links the trays. This connecting bar pivots around a central fulcrum, mediating the polarity of the trays. When the trays are "in balance," the opposites are held in dynamic equilibrium, and activity ceases. To achieve balance we need polarity but we also need something that mediates the polarity.

We have seen that The Opening Address and The College Founding have similar structures. We can imagine this structure as a scale with two trays containing the tasks of the individual teachers and of the school. Between them is the connecting bar—the collective work that we must do. We can also imagine those two addresses together on a scale, with The Opening Address on one side and The College Founding on the other. This scale balances the earthly tasks of the College with its spiritual tasks. The connecting bar is the collegial work of the teachers and their work with the spiritual worlds.

The image of the balance finds its correspondence in the structure of the first Goetheanum with its great hall composed of two intersecting domes. As Henry Barnes pointed out in *The Third Space*, the structure of the first Goetheanum expressed the polarity between the earthly and the cosmic, the sensible and the supersensible, the exoteric and the esoteric. Between the spaces of the hall and the stage was a "Third Space" created by the intersection of the two domes. In that space the earthly and the spiritual found their balance. Beyond that space, at the back of the stage, was to stand the statue of the Christ, the Representative of Humanity, who helps us achieve cosmic and earthly balance.

In the constellation Libra, Astraea, the goddess of earthly justice, holds the scales. So too the College of Teachers holds the scales by which the earthly and spiritual tasks of the school are balanced. As members of the College we need to be the balance in the school, but even more than that, we need to transform the word *balance* from noun into verb and thereby find the dynamic equilibrium between our tasks.

Our Tasks in Light of the Tasks of the Original College of Teachers

I think that the original group of teachers serves as the prototype for any College of Teachers. Their tasks are our tasks, and we can view our work in light of what Rudolf Steiner presented in The Opening Address and in The College Founding.

Goals: In The Opening Address Rudolf Steiner presented the original College of Teachers with three goals: to achieve a renewal of modern spiritual life; to reform and revolutionize the educational system; and to accomplish a great cultural deed. In The College Founding he also presented the teachers with three goals: to view their task as a moral spiritual task; to recognize the importance of their work; and to be conscious that this school fulfills something special.

These goals are just as apt today as they were in 1919. We are still trying to renew education. In order to do that we still need to recognize how special a Waldorf school is and to recognize the importance of our work. The College in every school needs to hold such goals in order to help its school and the Waldorf movement as a whole accomplish a great cultural deed: the renewal of modern spiritual life. How we go about this depends on the time and place in which we live and work. It is up to each College to try to read the signs of the times and the needs of its community and the wider culture to determine how the school can serve its lofty goals.

Anthroposophy: In The Opening Address Rudolf Steiner spoke about the relationship of anthroposophy to The Waldorf School. He told the teachers that The Waldorf School would be living proof of the effectiveness of the anthroposophical orientation toward life. It would accomplish this by being a unified school[3] that considered how to teach only in the way required by the human being.

In The College Founding Steiner revealed how anthroposophy can be brought to earth: by creating a connection between our activity and the activity of spiritual beings. He encouraged teachers to be conscious that they do not work only in the physical plane of living human beings, and he characterized the founding of The Waldorf School as a ceremony held within the Cosmic Order.

Strengthening the anthroposophical foundations of Waldorf education remains as important today as it was when the first Waldorf school was founded. The College must serve as the font of inspiration for the processes by which teachers can learn how to "transform what is gained through anthroposophy into truly practical instruction." It must support these processes through study, through artistic activity, and through the opportunities and means for anthroposophical professional development.

Steiner described the founding of The Waldorf School as a ceremony within the Cosmic Order. I think that the founding of every subsequent Waldorf school also has cosmic significance. Just as we celebrate the birth of a child because a soul-spiritual being has chosen to enter the earthly realm, we may celebrate the founding of a Waldorf school because it strives to bring the soul-spiritual into the realm of human life. This feeling of celebration should also permeate the founding of the College, and it can extend to each College meeting because during our meetings we can experience ourselves as working within the Cosmic Order to midwife the birth of spirit into matter.

Context: In The Opening Address Steiner described the difficult social and educational context in which The Waldorf School was being founded:

> The state imposes terrible learning goals and terrible standards, the worst imaginable, but people will imagine them to be the best. Today's policies and political activity treat people like pawns. More than ever before, attempts will be made to use people like cogs in a wheel. People will be handled like puppets on a string, and everyone will think that this reflects the greatest progress imaginable. Things like institutions of learning will be created incompetently and with the greatest arrogance.

Much of this description still holds true today. Although most Waldorf schools are ostensibly free from "terrible learning goals and terrible standards," these goals and standards permeate our culture. They establish expectations among the parents and the community and often become the standard against which Waldorf teachers are measured and against which they judge themselves. Standardized educational materials and the behavioral methods that are almost universally applied in other schools find their ways into our schools too.

As Waldorf teachers, we need to be informed about and to understand the prevailing view of the human being. We must be careful, however, not to allow that view to erode our recognition that the child is a spiritual being who has come to earth to do what it was not possible to do in the spiritual world. The College is the place where this view of the human being is broadened and deepened. The College strives to serve as the source of the strength and inspiration for teachers who are trying to "teach in the way required by the human being." By keeping the school's focus on the becoming human being, the College remains true to its intention.

Compromises: Steiner told the original teachers that they would have to make compromises. They would have to know their ideals and have the flexibility to conform to what lies far from those ideals. This remains true for us today as well. Every Waldorf school exists in a context—a community, a state, a country, a contemporary society—and it must adapt to that context through positive, creative, realistic means. It behooves us to emulate Steiner's calm, objective attitude towards this challenge. Rather than bemoan our situation, Waldorf teachers and Waldorf schools must embrace the opportunities and challenges of our time. We must love the age in which we and our students have incarnated because it presents us with exactly what we came to meet on earth.

The College should be the place in the school where a sense of contemporaneity is cultivated, where teachers are helped to become true citizens of the time and place into which they have incarnated. The challenges posed to us by the parents, our communities, and our culture provide us with the opportunities to develop the flexibility and strength that we need to create a truly modern art of education. If the College can stay true to its vision while adapting to its challenges, it will serve as a model that students will emulate in their adult lives.

Qualities: In The Opening Address and at the end of the preparatory course, Rudolf Steiner described the qualities and attitudes that Waldorf teachers should cultivate. Imagination, courage for the truth, responsibility of soul, initiative, interest in the world, integrity, and freshness of soul—these are the seven "virtues" that the Waldorf teacher strives to practice.[4]

Waldorf teachers practice these virtues in and out of the classroom in the service of their students. They practice these virtues in the College in service to each other and to the school. They are helped to do so by the Angels, Archangels, and Archai, who grant them the strength, courage, and light to do their work. By creating a true "Philadelphia," a city of brotherly love, in their meetings, members of the College further the work of the Good Spirit of the Time and of the Spirit of the Waldorf School.

The tasks of the original College of The Waldorf School of 1919 remain relevant for every College in every school today and into the future. During the two weeks of the preparatory course, Rudolf Steiner helped the teachers recognize and embrace these tasks. In our Colleges throughout the years, we have the honor of continuing to work on these tasks.

The Teachers' Republic

In the middle section of The Opening Address, Rudolf Steiner spoke about how The Waldorf School would be organized and administered, and what the teachers could do to develop a spirit of unity:

> Therefore, we will organize the school not bureaucratically, but collegially, and will administer it in a republican way. In a true teachers' republic, we will not have the comfort of receiving directions from the Board of Education. Rather, we must bring to our work what gives each of us the possibility and the full responsibility for what we have to do. Each one of us must be completely responsible.

> We can create a replacement for the supervision of the School Board as we form this preparatory course and, through the work, receive what unifies the school. We can achieve that sense of unity through this course if we work with all diligence.[5]

These important passages have been repeatedly analyzed over the years, and the many forms of administration and governance in Waldorf schools show that there are many ways to interpret them. I will examine these passages in terms of the work of the College of Teachers, but I believe that it is the responsibility of each College to understand and apply Rudolf Steiner's ideas as they pertain to its school. To me, the four essential ideas contained in these passages are:

1. The teachers are integral to the organization and administration of the school.
2. Each person needs to act with full responsibility.
3. We can create a replacement for direction or supervision from educational authorities.
4. We can work together in a way that unifies the school.

Let us examine each of these ideas.

1. *The teachers are integral to the organization and administration of the school.* Rudolf Steiner saw schools as organizations in the cultural sphere, which should be as free as possible from political control and economic constraints. Schools' top priority should be the educational process, and they should be organized and governed accordingly. In 1919 Steiner developed these ideas in *Basic Issues of the Social Question.* In the Preface he summarized the role of the teachers in administration:

> The administration of education, from which all culture develops, must be turned over to the educators. Economic and political considerations should be entirely excluded from this administration. Teachers should arrange their time so that they can also be administrators in their field. They should be just as much at home attending to administrative matters as they are in the classroom. No one should make decisions that is not directly engaged in the educational process. No parliament or congress, nor any individual who was perhaps once an educator, is to have anything to say. What is experienced in the teaching process would then flow naturally into the administration. By its very nature such a system would engender competence and objectivity.[6]

According to Steiner, schools must not lose sight of their most important function: education. To serve that function, a school's organization and administration need to be informed by those closest to the educational process. This will allow what is experienced in teaching to flow into administration. In my opinion, whether or not teachers should participate directly in administration needs to be determined by each school according to its circumstances. But having teachers who are as much at home tending to administrative matters as to teaching in the classroom helps keep a school focused on its mission of educating children. The College in every school needs to find the proper balance between the educational and administrative realms. If the College views these as two faces of the same coin, then the school's operations will be illuminated by pedagogical insight and the work of the teachers will be enhanced by practical, effective administration and management.

2. *Each person needs to act in full responsibility.* In order to act with full responsibility, we need to identify to whom we are responsible. I think that those of us who work in a Waldorf school are responsible to many: to ourselves, to the students and their families, to our colleagues, to the school and its community, and to the spiritual beings who are involved in our school. In a larger sense, I think we are also responsible to the nation in which we live, to the needs of our times, and to the earth and the spiritual worlds. If everyone who works in a Waldorf school recognizes and accepts this, then working in full responsibility means being aware of our own place in the cosmos as agents for the course of earth evolution.

The College needs to support this view of concentric circles of responsibility and help its members shoulder those responsibilities according to their abilities. This means that the College has to determine how much its members can or should do and how much needs to be delegated. Delegation does not mean, however, that we are no longer fully responsible; rather, it means that we are not necessarily responsible for the execution of a task. When individuals or groups act on behalf of the College or the school, they need to know that the College bears the ultimate responsibility for what they do. Because so much of what happens in a Waldorf school is done on behalf of the

College, the processes of delegating and sharing responsibility are among the College's most important tasks.

3. *We can create a replacement for direction or supervision from educational authorities.* In educational systems that have a School Board or Board of Education, the Board establishes the school's educational goals and determines the staffing, facilities, and programs by which these goals can be achieved. In The Waldorf School, these responsibilities were put into the hands of the individual teachers and the "teachers' republic." Through the preparatory course Rudolf Steiner planned to lay the foundation for the teachers' understanding of the nature of the human being and the needs of the developing child, and he intended to outline the curriculum and the methods that would best serve the educational process. He did this not only to prepare the teachers for their pedagogical tasks but also to help them to become co-creative and co-responsible for the education and for the school.

I believe that Rudolf Steiner intended for teachers— as individuals and as a group—to replace the educational authorities by becoming their own authority. This authority would be born out of proper preparation, continual review and reflection, and a willingness to develop and change in order to meet the needs of the students. If teachers are to be their own authority, they have to demonstrate their competence and be accountable. The College needs to cultivate a school culture that inspires and encourages the teachers' striving. The College also needs to support this striving by providing the circumstances and means for teacher preparation, effective procedures for review and evaluation, and mentoring or peer supervision at all levels.

Rudolf Steiner said, "We can create a replacement for the supervision of the School Board *as we form this preparatory course*" (emphasis added). I believe the forming of the preparatory course referred to what he would be presenting in The College Founding. In that presentation, Rudolf Steiner urged teachers to form a connection with the spiritual powers. If we form this connection, we allow the beings of the Third Hierarchy to "direct" and "supervise" us. These beings show us what is needed and they give us what we need to do our work. If we work with our Angel, we are given the strength to perform our tasks and to work on ourselves in service to our students. In our work together with the Archangels, we are given the courage to receive and to give to one another what we have developed in our individual work in service to our school. In our work with the Archai, we are given the light to perceive the needs of our time in service to the world.

4. *We can work together in a way that unifies the school.* Rudolf Steiner told the participants in the preparatory course that they would receive what would unify the school if they worked with due diligence. What was presented in this course and how does that allow a sense of unity to be achieved?

In the opening morning lectures Rudolf Steiner presented a description of the human being from the psychological, spiritual, and physical perspectives (*Study of Man*). Later in the morning he gave an overview of the curriculum in the light of child development and described teaching methods for each stage of development (*Practical Advice to Teachers*). In the afternoon seminar Rudolf Steiner gave further curricular indications, describing and demonstrating how some of the subjects might be taught (*Discussions with Teachers*).

The preparatory course was intended to prepare the founding teachers for their pedagogical tasks. Their work with it was intended to engender a sense of unity which would allow the teachers to govern themselves and to guide the school. Here is how I think a spirit of unity can be achieved by working with the preparatory course: When teachers work individually with the preparatory course, they unite themselves with other teachers who are also working on the course. This creates a community of ideas, of Imaginations. When teachers work as a group with the preparatory course, they unite themselves with all other groups who are working with the course. This creates a community of ideals, of Inspirations. When teachers work with the spiritual beings on the intentions of the preparatory course, they unite themselves with the Good Spirit of the Time to bring Waldorf education into earthly form. This creates a community of moral deeds, of Intuitions. These forms of working together are strengthened by working with the College Imagination, which will be described in a later section of this article.

I think that Rudolf Steiner did not elaborate further on the work of the teachers with each other because that kind of work would need to be determined together. It was up to the College to realize (i.e., make real) the ideas and ideals that Rudolf Steiner had shared. Every College has this charge: to figure out how teachers can work in full responsibility and in a way that unifies the school. Like any art, the art of self-governance needs to be practiced to achieve its goal: the administration, management, and leadership of a school that truly serves the education of the child.

II. Who Serves on the College of Teachers?

The College is composed of members of the school staff who are committed to working collegially on behalf of the school. In order to serve on a College, a person will typically have been confirmed in his or her work in the school, intends to work at the school into the foreseeable future, is willing to commit him- or herself to upholding the College's processes, and works with anthroposophy as his or her spiritual path.

In most schools the College is composed primarily of teachers. This makes sense because they are most directly involved in the education of students and can keep the education as the central focus of all of the school's functions. Over the years it has been suggested that College membership should be restricted to teachers because they develop special qualities through their work with the children and because the spiritual world expresses itself so directly through children, which helps the teacher perceive what may be needed for the future. I do not think that College membership should be restricted to teachers. While working with the children certainly demands that we grow and develop ourselves, every vocation offers opportunities for growth and self-development. Someone who does not work with children develops other qualities and perspectives, and the College can benefit from these. Even the first Waldorf school included members who were not teachers because they had a special reason for participating.

The College of the first Waldorf school included those people whom Rudolf Steiner invited to participate in the preparatory course who went on to work at the school. As additional teachers were hired, questions arose about whether all the teachers should participate in the College. At the end of the first school year, in the meeting with the teachers on July 30, 1920, Rudolf Steiner said:

> It is certainly not so that we will include every specialty teacher in the faculty [*Lehrerkollegium*]. The intent is that the inner faculty [*engeres Kollegium*] includes the class teachers and the older specialty teachers, and that we also have an extended faculty [*erweiterte Kollegium*]. …Only the main teachers, those who are practicing, not on leave, should be on the faculty. In principle, the faculty should consist of those who originally were part of the school and

those who came later but who we wish had participated in the course last year. We have always discussed who is to be here as a real teacher. If someone is to sit with us, he or she must be practicing and must be a true teacher.

When Berta Molt said that she didn't belong there, Rudolf Steiner replied:

You are the school mother. That was always the intent. Mrs. Steiner is here as the head of the eurythmy department and Mr. Molt as the patron of the school; that was always the intent from the very beginning.[7]

In order to understand more fully who should serve on the College, let us examine what Rudolf Steiner presented in the preparatory course.

Qualities and Criteria for College Members

What are the qualities that College members should have and develop? In The Opening Address Rudolf Steiner spoke about the qualities that teachers would need in order to do their work. They correspond closely to the qualities that he spoke about at the end of the course. In The College Founding Rudolf Steiner presented seven other qualities that have to do with the spiritual work of the teachers. Here again the image of the balance arises. In the two trays are the qualities that are needed by teachers to do their earthly tasks, in the middle the qualities needed by teachers to perform their spiritual tasks together.

The qualities outlined here are needed by anyone who intends to work in the earthly and in the spiritual realms as individuals and as a group. The qualities from the beginning and at the end of the course (the outer columns) are addressed to us as individuals, while those presented in The College

Founding (the middle column) address us as a group. Members of the College must take up their individual work, but they also have a collective task because only where two or more are gathered is it possible to work directly with the higher spiritual powers.

The Council of the Pedagogical Section of the School of Spiritual Science in North America established the following criteria for participation as a member of a College of Teachers. The person should

1. be confirmed in his or her work in the school
2. intend to work at the school into the foreseeable future
3. commit him- or herself to upholding the College's processes
4. be working with anthroposophy as his or her spiritual path

Let us review these criteria for College membership in terms of what Rudolf Steiner put forth in The College Founding and in the faculty meeting of July 30, 1920, quoted previously.

1. *The person has been confirmed in his or her work in the school.* This criterion corresponds to Rudolf Steiner's injunction that the person view his or her work as a moral and spiritual task and be a "true" teacher.

2. *The person intends to work at the school into the foreseeable future.* This corresponds to Rudolf Steiner's description of the original teachers as individuals brought together by karma who were working together in the Cosmic Order as well as those who were part of the school in the beginning or who were wished to have participated.

3. *The person commits him- or herself to upholding the processes of the College.* This criterion corresponds to Rudolf Steiner's description of a teacher as someone who will work with

Opening Address	College Founding	Final Words
1. Know your ideals	View our work as a moral spiritual task	"Imbue thyself with the power of imagination"
2. Have the flexibility to conform to what lies far from your ideals	Reflect on the connection between your activity and the spiritual worlds	"Have courage for the truth"
3. Be completely responsible	Work with the spiritual powers	"Sharpen thy feeling for responsibility of soul"
4. Be conscious of the great tasks	See the importance of our work	Be a person of initiative
5. Have a living interest in the world	View the founding of this school as a ceremony held within the Cosmic Order	Have an interest in everything in the world
6. Obtain enthusiasm for our school and our tasks	See each other as human beings brought together by karma	Never compromise with what is untrue
7. Develop flexibility of spirit and devotion to our tasks	More that will be said at the end of the course	Never grow stale or sour; cultivate freshness of soul

colleagues in the "teacher's republic" and in the esoteric collegial work described in the College Imagination.*

4. *The person is working with anthroposophy as his or her spiritual path.* This criterion corresponds to Rudolf Steiner's description in The College Founding in which he characterizes how we connect with the spiritual powers and how we work with the College Imagination and the Teachers Meditation(s).

The work of the College is very demanding on the earthly and spiritual levels. These criteria ensure that a person who serves on a College will have the foundation necessary to attempt to participate in the College. Although none of us is fully qualified, our intention and our striving will bind us to our colleagues and attract the spiritual beings who wish to help us with our work.

Anthroposophy as the College Member's Spiritual Path

The following questions are often posed with regard to service on a College: Does a member of the College need to be an anthroposophist? Does he or she need to be a member of the Anthroposophical Society or of the Pedagogical Section or the First Class of the School of Spiritual Science?** I think that

---

*In some Colleges, this criterion includes the commitment to upholding confidentiality. The word *confidence* stems from the Latin root *fidere*, which means "to trust." It is also connected to the word *fidelity*, which derives from the Latin root for "faith." When we commit to confidentiality, we commit ourselves to trusting and remaining faithful to each other and, I believe, to the spiritual beings with whom we are trying to work.

**The School of Spiritual Science is the part of the Anthroposophical Society that works with the meditative content which Rudolf Steiner shared in the "Class Lessons." Anyone can join the Anthroposophical Society who recognizes the validity of anthroposophy and of the Goetheanum as the center for anthroposophical activities, but in order to join the School of Spiritual Science, one must also be willing to represent and defend anthroposophy. The Pedagogical Section is one of the vocational sections of the School of Spiritual Science.

these questions deserve consideration, but the most appropriate perspective will be gleaned by a group of colleagues who consider these questions in the context of their own school. The process of arriving at a common position on such questions brings colleagues together in a way that serves the school.

I do not think that membership in the Anthroposophical Society or the School of Spiritual Science should be required for College membership. Membership in these groups must be based on the principle of freedom, and if a person were to be required to join in order to be eligible for College membership, it would compromise that principle. Joining the School of Spiritual Science expresses a person's willingness to represent and defend anthroposophy; it should not qualify a person for College membership. The Anthroposophical Society and the School of Spiritual Science benefit when a person joins and supports them, but that participation should arise out of a gesture of giving rather than taking. The requirements for College membership that have been described are stringent enough; there is not need to add to them.

While College membership should not depend on whether a person is a "card-carrying anthroposophist," I am convinced that whoever intends to serve on a College must be working with anthroposophy as his or her spiritual path and way of life. Unless anthroposophy firmly underlies a College member's worldview, he or she will not be effective in helping the Waldorf school serve as "living proof of the effectiveness of the anthroposophical orientation toward life." This applies particularly to teaching because Waldorf education is a practical utilization of anthroposophy and it is the teacher's goal to "transform what we can gain through anthroposophy into truly practical instruction." Rudolf Steiner stressed the importance of anthroposophy in his final message to the teachers in 1925, when he said that the Waldorf school is "a visible sign of the fruitfulness of anthroposophy within the spiritual life of mankind."[8]

Those who serve on the College strive to bring anthroposophy to life through the College work. This is most evident in one's work with the College Imagination. The College Imagination was not intended simply as imaginative content for contemplation; it was intended to be used by the teachers in their work on themselves, with the children, and with one another. Working on the College also requires members to try to create the conditions for what Rudolf Steiner called "the reverse ritual," which will be described later. The reverse ritual is built on a foundation of shared idealism. It is fostered through a study and practice of anthroposophy, creating a "common language" that supports community building and a connection to spiritual beings.

I believe that a person working in a Waldorf school must be entirely free to pursue his or her own spiritual path without any kind of judgment or sanction, but there is a big difference between working in a Waldorf school and serving on the College. Working as a member of the College demands fidelity to anthroposophy and to shared meditative work that springs from anthroposophy. Without these, the College will find it very difficult to serve as a bridge between the spiritual world and the earthly world of human beings.

Every school has to develop the processes by which individuals can identify themselves or be recognized as striving to meet these criteria. It is important, however, that College membership not be viewed as a matter of status but as a matter of service, of being willing to make the sacrifices that are required to work together. We cannot confirm ourselves in our work; we have to be confirmed by our colleagues. We cannot commit ourselves to working by ourselves with the destiny of our school; karma demands that we work with others. College work is group work, and it can occur only when a person is recognized in relationship to the group and when the group demonstrates its regard for the person.

Whenever a College welcomes a new member, the possibility arises for the College to reconnect to the College Founding of 1919, to celebrate a festive moment in the Cosmic Order. The welcoming ceremony provides an opportunity for the College to re-affirm its roots, to acknowledge its connections to the College members who have passed the Threshold, and to strengthen its commitment to work with spiritual powers. Such a ceremony is also a time to reconnect to Rudolf Steiner, who pledged to remain connected to the work of The Waldorf School.

Our Connection to Rudolf Steiner

Everyone who works in Waldorf education is connected to Rudolf Steiner in some way, but those who serve on the College need to deepen their connection to the man and his work so that they can continue to receive his help and he can continue to participate in continuing development of Waldorf education.

At the end of the preparatory course, Rudolf Steiner spoke to the teachers about his relationship to the teachers and to the school:

When you look back in memory to these discussions, then our thoughts will certainly meet again in all the various impulses that have come to life during this time. For myself, I can assure you that I will also be thinking back to these days, because right now this Waldorf school is indeed weighing heavily on the minds of those taking part in its beginning and organization. This Waldorf school must succeed; much depends on its success. Its success will bring a kind of proof of many things in the spiritual evolution of humankind that we must represent.

In conclusion, if you will allow me to speak personally for a moment, I would like to say: For me this Waldorf school will be a veritable child of concern. Again and again I will have to come back to this Waldorf school with anxious, caring thoughts. But when we keep in mind the deep seriousness of the situation, we can really work well together. Let us especially keep before us the thought, which will truly fill our hearts and minds, that connected with the present-day spiritual movement are also the spiritual powers that guide the cosmos. When we believe in these good spiritual powers, they will inspire our lives and we will truly be able to teach.[9]

For five years Rudolf Steiner worked with the teachers in the school, visiting classes, attending College meetings, speaking at assemblies and festivals, and presenting additional courses on education. When he became ill in 1924, he wrote to the teachers one last time, reaffirming his connection to them.

Rudolf Steiner is able to remain connected to Waldorf education through our relationship to him. Like every relationship, it takes work to keep it strong and vibrant. We can strengthen our relationship to Rudolf Steiner by continuing to work with anthroposophy, bringing it to life in us and through us.

In *The Christmas Foundation: Beginning of a New Cosmic Age*, Rudolf Grosse refers to an essay by Ita Wegman which quotes Rudolf Steiner as saying that if after his death "the opposition forces then succeed in separating anthroposophy from me by allowing the broad masses of humanity to hear of the teaching without knowing anything about me, it would become superficial, and this would be just what the Ahrimanic beings want and intend."[10]

As Rudolf Steiner's life recedes into the distances of time, it will also become increasingly possible to speak about Waldorf education with diminishing reference to him. If this occurs, Waldorf education will suffer by losing its integrity and becoming just another educational philosophy and method. We can prevent this from happening by continuing to affirm Rudolf Steiner's role as the founder of Waldorf education. This does not mean that we need to exalt or deify Rudolf Steiner, but we must continue to acknowledge his contribution. When the College cultivates its relationship to Rudolf Steiner, it gives him the opportunity to continue to help us and guide us in our work.

When Should a School Found the College of Teachers?

Most Waldorf schools in North America found a College only when the school has reached a certain level of maturity. Until that time, various individuals and groups carry the responsibilities that the College will eventually assume.

I have long held that a College should be founded before or when a school opens rather than as a later development. Because the College is essential to the work of a Waldorf school, to wait until a school has reached a certain degree of maturity misses the opportunity to work with the spiritual powers right from the start. The College is the place in the school where the spiritual impulses that are trying to manifest in the school can do so most directly. It is the place where a balance is sought between the earthly realms and the spiritual realms. I think that a school benefits from developing that place from its inception so that it can become firmly grounded in the school's way of working.

This does not mean that a new or young College is ready to govern, administer, or manage a new school. Even a mature College may choose not to perform all of these tasks. Rather, a College—young or mature—needs to make sure that the major decisions about the school are permeated with the goals and values of the education. In the early years of a school, when its Board of Trustees is engaged in many aspects of operations and management, the College has a special opportunity to develop the spiritual aspects of group work so that when it begins to shoulder more earthly tasks, the group will be strong enough to meet the challenges.

If a school waits to found a College, how do the spiritual beings participate in the work of the teachers? It seems to me that the lack of a College makes this more difficult. Rudolf Steiner characterized the work of these beings in the College Imagination. There he described how each of us works with our Angel, who gives us strength. This work does not depend on a College. The work that we do with our Angels is taken up by the Archangels, who work together to create a chalice of courage. I believe that even without a College, the Archangels will perform this work, but it may be harder for the group to experience it and to feel unified by it. The College Imagination describes how the Archai allow a drop of light to fill the chalice formed by the movements of the Archangels. This light serves as a beacon for the group, giving it the wisdom to take up its tasks. If there is no College, I can imagine that this light will not be experienced as fully.

Whether a school founds its College early on or later in its biography, its members must take up the challenge of working together productively with one another and with spiritual beings. Only by meeting this challenge can the College fulfill its task to serve as a bridge and a balance between the worlds of matter and spirit.

The Challenge of Working Together

One of the major goals of Waldorf education is to help students become individuals in the context of a group. The College tries to exemplify this dynamic; its members try to work in a way that allows the capacities of each individual to serve the group, which in turn recognizes and utilizes those capacities. A verse by Rudolf Steiner points to the balance that must be achieved in order for an individual to work as a member of a group.

> *The healthy social life is found*
> *When, in the mirror of each human soul,*
> *The whole community finds its reflection*
> *And when, in the community,*
> *The virtue of each one is living.*[11]

Working in the College depends on the striving of the members to wake up to one another so that they can recognize each other in the deepest sense. Out of that recognition comes the possibility for delegation and for shared responsibility. When Rudolf Steiner spoke about a republican form of administration, he was identifying a way of working together that allows each person to be fully responsible for his own work and for the group to share the responsibility for the work as a whole.

Any group trying to work together faces many challenges, some in the earthly realm and some in the spiritual. While the earthly challenges are unique to each school, all schools face similar spiritual challenges because they are the result of the work of two beings who take special interest in human beings. According to Rudolf Steiner, Lucifer and Ahriman are spiritual beings who play a special role in human affairs. They are especially attracted to a group such as a College in a Waldorf school, since it is working for the further development of human beings and society. It is easy to think of Lucifer and Ahriman as being merely adversarial forces or the embodiment of evil, but both of these beings are necessary for our full development.

Ahriman is deeply connected to physical, material existence. His influence can be found wherever earthly matters are most important. The realms of science and technology, government and economics, industry and the military have developed in accordance with Ahrimanic forms of thinking and working. Ahrimanic thinking is clear and logical; work inspired by Ahriman is realistic and pragmatic; goals can justify means. In groups, Ahriman expresses himself through the principle of power, and groups that are inspired by Ahriman have a strictly hierarchical organization. Ahriman's cosmic intention is to keep human beings from developing their spiritual nature. If Ahriman were to succeed, we would remain purely physical beings tied to the earth and governed by our passions and needs.

When we consider practical matters in the College, Ahriman draws near. He can help us solve problems, but we must make sure that the solution is consistent with our values. He can help us streamline our operations, but we must make sure that our processes and procedures remain human. Ahriman can help us be more realistic, pragmatic, and decisive, which is necessary if the College is to work effectively, but we must be careful to keep his help in perspective and not depend on him too much.

Lucifer is connected to the world of the spirit. His influence can be found wherever ideas and ideals govern with little regard for the practicalities of life. His influence can be found in culture, in religion, in the arts, and in all forms of self-expression. Lucifer inspires creativity in thinking and working. In groups, he works through the principles of individual autonomy, personal initiative, and freedom from constraints. Lucifer's cosmic intention is to transform human beings into purely spiritual beings who would have no need to be incarnated into physical bodies. If Lucifer were to succeed, human beings would be drawn away from the earth to lead a purely spiritual existence as moral automatons.

When we consider spiritual matters in the College, Lucifer draws near. He can help us develop insights into a problem, but we must make sure we don't lose sight of the need to find a timely solution. He can help us humanize our operations, but we must make sure that our processes and procedures are not derailed by personal consideration. Lucifer can help us be receptive and responsive—which is necessary if the College is to work with sensitivity—but we must be careful to keep his help in perspective and not to depend on him too much.

We need Ahriman and Lucifer in order to perform the earthly and spiritual tasks of our schools, but we must remain awake to these beings' one-sidedness and their intention to deprive us of our essential humanity. As members of the College, we need to find our place between Lucifer and Ahriman, where we can strive to be true to ourselves, to each other, and to the highest intentions of the spiritual worlds.

According to Rudolf Steiner, the being who holds Lucifer and Ahriman in a dynamic balance is the Christ. Rudolf Steiner represented the relationship between the Christ and humanity's great adversaries in the great wooden statue that was to stand at the back of the stage of the great hall under the small dome of the first Goetheanum. The statue depicts the Christ, the Representative of Humanity, reaching upward with one hand, holding Lucifer at bay and reaching downward with the other hand, keeping Ahriman in his place. The Christ holds the adversaries at arm's length, allowing them to do their necessary work while he continues to stride forward toward his goal.

The statue of the *Representative of Humanity* provides a picture of the balance that we must strive to achieve: holding

Lucifer and Ahriman in a dynamic balance, a balance in which each of these beings can share his gifts but also be held in check so that his excesses do not harm us. If we become true co-workers of the Christ, He will help us to achieve this balance in ourselves and in our work.

III. Why Is It Important for a Waldorf School to Have a College of Teachers?

A Waldorf school is more than an earthly institution; it also has a spiritual mission. In order for the Waldorf school to fulfill its mission, it needs to recognize the spiritual realities that stand behind it and provide a way for the spiritual beings who are trying to help humanity to participate in earthly matters. A College serves as a conduit to and from the spiritual world. Without this living link to the spiritual world, a Waldorf school will find it difficult to perceive and express the will of spiritual beings.

Rudolf Steiner described the work of the Waldorf teachers with the spiritual hierarchies most directly in The College Founding, but in various other lectures he also dealt with this topic. It is useful to examine some of these indications because they shed light on our work as a College.

Building Community

In 1905, Rudolf Steiner gave a lecture entitled "Brotherhood and the Fight for Survival" (Berlin, November 23, 1905). In this lecture he spoke about the need for community building, and he described how spiritual beings act through communities of people who are working together towards an ideal.

Union—community—means that a higher being presses itself through the unified members. It is a universal principle of life; five people, who are together, who think and feel harmoniously together in common, are more than one plus one plus one plus one plus one. ...A new higher being is among these five—even among two or three: "Where two or three are gathered together in My name, there I am among them." It is not the one or the other or the third, but something entirely new that comes into appearance through the unification, but it comes about only if the individual lives in the other one—if the single one obtains his powers not only from himself but also out of the others. It can happen only if each of us lives selflessly in the others.

Thus human communities are mystery places where higher spiritual beings descend to act through the individual human beings, just as the soul expresses itself in the members of the body. ...One cannot see the spirits who live in communities but they are there. They are there because of the sisterly, brotherly love of the personalities working in these communities. As the body has a soul, so a guild or community also has a soul, and I repeat, it is not spoken allegorically but must be taken as a full reality.

Those who work together in mutual help are magicians because they pull in higher beings. One does not call upon the machinations of spiritism if one works together in a community in sisterly, brotherly love. Higher beings manifest themselves there. If we give up ourselves to mutual help, through this giving up to the community a powerful strengthening of our organs takes place. If we then speak or act as a member of such a community, there speaks or acts in us not the singular soul only but the spirit of the community. This is the secret of progress for the future of mankind: to work out of communities.[12]

It is interesting to note that long before the founding of the first Waldorf school, Rudolf Steiner was already speaking to the need to found communities out of the spirit, out of the highest ideals of the soul. "We must learn to lead community life," he said. "We shall not believe that the one or the other is able to accomplish anything by him- or herself."[13]

In 1923, four years after the Waldorf School was founded, Rudolf Steiner returned to the theme of community building in a group of lectures published as *Awakening to Community*. In Lectures 6 and 9 he describes how communities can attract and engage spiritual beings, a process that is integral to the work of the College.

The Reverse Ritual

If the College is to be a true spiritual community bound by spiritual idealism, its members need to work in a way that attracts spiritual beings to participate in its tasks. In *Awakening to Community*, Rudolf Steiner describes how this can be done.

Community life is based on different types of common experience. The broadest foundation for community is language, which creates a connection among all who share a mother tongue. The second foundation for community is provided by our shared childhood experiences and our memories of them. They create a sense of connection among those who have shared their early lives. The third foundation for community is common participation in rituals. According to Rudolf Steiner, a "cultus" or true ritual is an earthly reflection of something we have experienced in the spiritual world before birth. When we participate in a ritual together, we feel a connection with those who are participating with us because we have common cosmic memories of the experiences from our time before birth.

A true ritual, Rudolf Steiner states, "derives its binding power from the fact that it conveys spiritual forces from the spiritual world to earth and presents supernatural realities to the contemplation of human beings living on the earth."[14] An individual usually decides whether to participate in a ritual, but rituals can easily become tradition, which causes us to engage in them less consciously.

The fourth foundation for community is what Rudolf Steiner terms the "reverse cultus" or "reverse ritual." This foundation is not given to us; it must be established consciously at every moment. The reverse ritual can occur only when we truly awaken to the soul and spiritual nature of our fellow man. According to Rudolf Steiner, when we begin to awaken to one another in this way, we are able to enter the supersensible realm together.

This awakening to each other's soul-spiritual nature can occur by sharing a common life of ideals. This attracts the interest of spiritual beings. When we seek to realize our anthroposophical ideals, a spiritual being is attracted to our work. "Just as the genius of a language lives in that language and spreads its wings over those who speak it, so do those who experience anthroposophical ideas together in the right, idealistic frame of mind live in the shelter of the wings of a higher being."[15] This process of spiritualizing earthly substance together is the reverse ritual.

While a ritual brings the supersensible down into the physical world through words and actions, the reverse ritual raises earthly deeds into the supersensible realm. Rudolf Steiner described it pictorially as follows:

> The community of the cultus seeks to draw the Angels of heaven down to the place where the cultus is being celebrated, so that they may be present in the congregation,

whereas the anthroposophical community seeks to lift human souls into supersensible realms so that they may enter the company of Angels.

If anthroposophy is to serve man as a real means of entering the spiritual world, …we must do more than just talk about spiritual beings; we must look for the opportunities nearest at hand to enter their company.[16]

When we participate in the reverse ritual, spiritual beings are attracted to our spiritualized thoughts, feelings, and deeds and are able to participate in the earthly matters that we are raising into the realm of the spirit. Just as true rituals bring the life of the spirit into the realm of earth, the reverse ritual brings the life of the earth into the realm of spirit.

The reverse ritual is possible only if the members of the College are working on themselves and working together in a way that fosters an awakening to each other's soul-spiritual nature. This means that College members need to learn to see one another in a new light and to relate to one another in new ways. In order to awaken to our colleagues' soul-spiritual nature we must develop heightened interest in, compassion for, and commitment to one another. This requires dedication and persistence because we are so used to relationships based on our everyday selves. If we begin to awaken to each other, we will find new levels of connection that will allow us to work together not only on earth but in spiritual realms as well.

The reverse ritual is at the crux of College work. When a meeting achieves the reverse ritual, spiritual beings receive an offering of spiritualized earthly substance that is akin to the blessing that we receive when we partake of a sacrament. When the reverse ritual occurs, the will of the spiritual world may be perceived by the listening heart. What is finally voiced aloud by one or another member of the group goes far beyond the sum of the individual opinions or perspectives that have been expressed. In those moments, one feels humbled by the recognition that one is participating in something rare and holy: the transmutation of earthly thoughts, words, and deeds into spiritual substance.

The College Imagination

In order for the reverse ritual to be fruitful for our work as a College, we also have to cultivate the ability to perceive what the spiritual beings are trying to communicate so that we can hearken to the will of the spiritual worlds. This demands that we develop ourselves as meditants so that we, like Elijah, can awaken to the still, small voice of the spirit. It demands that we engage in meetings that are structured to allow us to perceive that voice of the spirit. And it demands that we develop the qualities of soul that will allow us to speak to and listen to each other in such a way that doesn't stifle the expression of the spirit.

In the College Imagination and the Final Words, Rudolf Steiner gave the members of the preparatory course the means by which to imagine, understand, and practice working together with the spiritual powers who help us in our work.

Thus, we wish to begin our preparation by first reflecting upon how we connect with the spiritual powers in whose service and in whose name each one of us must work. I ask you to understand these introductory words as a kind of prayer to those powers who stand behind us with Imagination, Inspiration, and Intuition as we take up this task.[17]

Rudolf Steiner asked that his words not be transcribed at that point, but three of the participants later wrote down their recollections of what he had said. [see Appendix] The accounts differ in terms of the level of detail they record, but they share the following essential elements:

Our Angel helps us with our individual work, in our strivings to realize our goals for this incarnation. In the Imagination Rudolf Steiner describes the Angel as standing behind us and laying hands on our head. Our Angel faces the same direction as we do—perhaps in recognition that it will stand by us as we meet our destiny—and it gives us the strength we need to do our tasks.

The Archangels help us in our work with one another. Rudolf Steiner describes the Archangels as circling above our heads, carrying from one to the other what arises out of our spiritual encounter with our Angel. Their movements create a chalice made of courage.

The Archai help us in our work to realize the goals of the Spirit of the Time. Rudolf Steiner describes their movements less exactly, saying only that they come from primal distances or the heights. The Archai allow a drop of light to fill the chalice created by the Archangels.

Rudolf Steiner shared this Imagination so that the participants of the course could recognize the essential elements of how to work with these spiritual beings. We work with our Angel on our own tasks; we work with the Archangels on our common tasks; we work with the Archai on the tasks of our age. The correspondences among the parts of the College Imagination are summarized in the table on the next page.

Working with meditative content must be an act of freedom, but when members of a group such as the College commit to working with the same content in an ongoing way, it strengthens the meditative work of each individual and the

	Angel	Archangels	Archai
BEING			
POSITION	Behind each member	Above our heads	From eternal beginnings
MOVEMENT	Stands	Circle	Come from a distance
GESTURE	Lays hands on head	Form a chalice; carry from one to the other what each has to give	Reveal themselves for a moment
ACTION	Gives strength	Gives courage	Allow a drop of light to fall into the chalice
CAPACITY	Imagination	Inspiration	Intuition

power of the meditation itself. In my opinion, becoming a member of a College requires a commitment to engage in a group meditative practice in service to one's colleagues and to the school. When all the members of a College make that commitment, the whole that is created is far greater than the sum of the parts.

Rudolf Steiner intended that teachers work with the *Imagination* as part of their daily meditative practice. During The College Founding he said, "At the end of our course I will say what I would like to say following today's festive commencement of our preparation. Then much will have been clarified, and we will be able to stand before our task much more concretely than we can today."[18] At the end of the last lectures, Rudolf Steiner spoke about the qualities that the teachers must develop. When he concluded the course, he described how teachers could work together with the beings of the Third Hierarchy, and he asked that the teachers pledge themselves to do this. According to the notes of Caroline von Heydebrand:

> On 9th September at 9am, Rudolf Steiner assembled the first Waldorf teachers. He asked them always to remember the way of working which he had shown to them, namely to work in full consciousness of the reality of the spiritual world. He said: "In the evenings *before* your meditation, ask the Angels, Archangels and Archai that they may help you in your work on the following day. In the mornings, *after* the meditation, you may feel yourself united with the beings of the Third Hierarchy."

> Then Dr. Steiner walked around the table, shaking hands with each teacher and looking deeply and with moving, utmost earnestness into the eyes of each.

According to the notes of Walter J. Stein:

> 9am meeting. Dr. Steiner asks us, clasping the hand of each
> teacher in turn, to promise to work together in the way he
> has shown us: In the evening, before the meditation, ask
> the Angeloi, Archangeloi and Archai to help in our work on
> the next day. In the morning, after the meditation, know
> ourselves united with them.[19]

Although we were not present at this ceremony, it lives on
as a cosmic moment in which we can participate through our
intentions and our efforts. Each us can receive what Rudolf
Steiner offered if we take up his work with earnestness, and each
of us can pledge to work in the way that he has shown. If we
do so, we connect ourselves with Rudolf Steiner and with the
Being of The Waldorf School.

The Being of The Waldorf School

In Waldorf circles people sometimes refer to the "being" of
their school. What is meant by that? Whom are they speaking
about? Is this simply a turn of phrase or does it point to a
spiritual reality?

According to Rudolf Steiner each human being has an
Angel who has the spiritual task of helping that human being
fulfill his or her pre-birth intentions. Archangels are on the next
higher level. They concern themselves with groups of people
who have basic background in common: a tribe, a race, people
from a geographical region, people who share a language. These
beings are sometimes known as the "folk-soul" of a people.
The Archai are one level above the Archangels. As Spirits of
the Time, they are responsible for the developments that occur
within an age. The major Archangels also may serve as the Spirit

of the Time for an epoch, and during this period of regency, they act as if they were in the ranks of the Archai.

What kind of spiritual being is "the being of the school?" In my opinion, there are two possibilities: If we view "the school" as a specific Waldorf school, I think the "being of the school" is one type of spiritual being. If we view "The Waldorf School" as an archetype, then I think the "Being of the School" is another type of spiritual being.

As Rudolf Steiner described in "Brotherhood and the Fight for Survival" and in *Awakening to Community*, wherever a group of people come together in the service of an ideal, a spiritual being is drawn to them. It seems to me that this being comes from the ranks of the Archangels, because the Archangels are responsible for and express themselves through a group of people.

The Archangels have the astral body as their lowest member, which allows them to manifest themselves in many places at once. Because the being of a school expresses itself through many members of the school community, this may explain why people in a school have the feeling that they speak a common language, share common values, and belong together.

The astral body can be thought of as a body of air. The air is common to us all, uniting us as we inhale each other's air. Because the air carries our voices, it unites us through our common language. When a school community sings or speaks together, united in its breathing, we can imagine the being of the school breathing through and with them.

The astral body also provides the foundation for our soul life, expressing itself through the personality. This "school personality" may be the earthly expression of the nature of its archangelic being. We can experience something of this being when we share our school's vision and values, participate in its customs and traditions, experience our community through the common ground of the school's biography.

By working to perceive the character of the school, by finding the common language—both spoken and unspoken—that unites the school, by seeking ways to recognize and utilize each other's gifts for the common good, the members of the College can get to know the being of their school and invite it to participate in their work.

"The Waldorf School" transcends all the individual Waldorf schools. It is an archetype that expresses itself throughout all the places and times where Waldorf education is being realized. When we review The Opening Address and The College Founding, we sense that Rudolf Steiner was inaugurating "The Waldorf School," not just a Waldorf school in Stuttgart. We sense that the festive moment in the Cosmic Order celebrated the beginning of something greater than the establishment of a particular school. When we read and work with Rudolf Steiner's words and ideas from the preparatory course, we sense that what he presented to those original teachers was being presented to Waldorf teachers in all places and times to come. If "The Waldorf School" is an archetype that expresses itself through the individual Waldorf schools, then the "Being of The Waldorf School" is on a higher level than the Archangels who are connected to the individual schools.

I think that the Being of The Waldorf School is The Good Spirit of the Time whom Rudolf Steiner thanked in The College Founding and referred to in the College Imagination as that spirit who bestows upon us the drop of light. Although he did not mention the Good Spirit by name, I think that Rudolf Steiner was referring to the Archangel Michael, who is serving in the ranks of the Archai during this age. Just as Archangels can manifest in different places at once, the Archai can manifest in different times at once. As the Spirit of the Time, Michael is able to manifest in all of the different Waldorf schools wherever and whenever they exist.

The Archangel Michael has a special connection to all who are involved in Waldorf education because we were already members in the School of Michael before our birth. In 1922, in the last lecture of *The Younger Generation*, Rudolf Steiner spoke about Michael in connection with education.

> Michael needs, as it were, a chariot by means of which to enter our civilization. And this chariot reveals itself to the true educator as coming forth from the young, growing human being, yes, even from the child. Here the power of the pre-earthly life is still working. Here we find, if we nurture it, what becomes the chariot by means of which Michael will enter our civilization. By educating in the right way, we are preparing Michael's chariot for entrance into our civilization.[20]

A year later, during the last lecture of *Deeper Insights into Waldorf Education*, presented to the teachers of the Waldorf School, Rudolf Steiner again stressed the importance of uniting oneself with Michael. Afterwards he presented the second Teachers Meditation, which gives teachers the means by which to connect more deeply with the spiritual wellsprings of their work.[21]

The College in a Waldorf school has the sacred duty to get to know and to work with the Archangel Michael. Through him the College can receive the drop of light that enlightens their work. Through him they can unite themselves with his mission to create a more human future. Through him they can experience more fully the Spirit of the Waldorf School.

The Spirit of the Waldorf School

The Being of the Waldorf School expresses and is the countenance of The Spirit of the Waldorf School. The Spirit of the Waldorf School expresses itself wherever two or more are gathered in their striving to realize the ideals of Waldorf education. Rudolf Steiner spoke explicitly about The Spirit of the Waldorf School in several of his assembly talks and festival addresses to students, teachers, and parents. At the Christmas assembly of the first school, Rudolf Steiner said to the children:

And do you know where your teachers get all the strength and ability they need so that they can teach you to grow up to be good and capable people? They get it from the Christ.[22]

At the assembly at the end of the first school year, he said:

There is still something I would like to say today. Alongside everything we have learned here, which the individual teachers have demonstrated so beautifully, there is something else present, something that I would like to call the Spirit of the Waldorf School. It is meant to lead us to true piety again. Basically, it is the spirit of Christianity that wafts through all our rooms, that comes from every teacher and goes out to every child, even when it seems that something very far from religion is being taught, such as arithmetic, for example. Here it is always the spirit of Christ that comes from the teacher and is to enter the hearts of the children—this spirit that is imbued with love, real human love.[23]

During the second school year, at the assembly of November 20, 1920, he said:

What your teachers say to you comes from incredibly hard work on their part, from the strength of their devotion and from their love for you. But what comes from their love must also be able to get to you, and that is why I always say the same thing to you: Love your teachers, because love will carry what comes from your teachers' hearts into your hearts and into your heads. Love is the best way for what teachers have to give to flow into their students. That is why I am going to ask you again today, "Do you love your teachers? Do you still love them?" [The children shout, "Yes!"]

A little later in this assembly, Rudolf Steiner said: "Thus the spirit of Christ is always with you. ...This spirit of Christ is also your teachers' great teacher. Through your teachers, the spirit of Christ works into your hearts."[24]

At the assembly marking the beginning of the sixth school year, Rudolf Steiner again mentioned the teachers' teacher:

Dear students of the highest grade of all—that is, dear teachers! In this new school year, let us begin teaching with courage and enthusiasm to prepare these children for the school of life. Thus may the school be guided by the greatest leader of all, by the Christ Himself. May this be the case in our school.[25]

When Rudolf Steiner visited the Waldorf School, he would ask the students, "Do you love your teachers?" and he would sometimes ask them several times. By asking this question Rudolf Steiner was helping the students and the teachers to recognize that without the love that streams from teacher to student and from student to teacher, no education is possible. Rudolf Steiner did not explicitly ask the students of the highest grade of all—the teachers—if they loved their teacher, but that question is implicit in all that we do as Waldorf teachers and as human beings living at this time. The Christ is the Spirit of the Waldorf School. If we are truly to serve Waldorf education, we must find our way to the Christ and learn to love Him.*

Conclusion

The College in a Waldorf school has a lofty task: to guide the school by finding a bridge and a balance between the earthly and the spiritual realms. It is composed of people who are committed to working together in recognition of their karma and their common spiritual striving. By working on their self-development and their relationships with one another, members of the College try to create the conditions for the reverse ritual. The College recognizes that it does not work alone. Its members strive to work with the being of their school and to connect to the Angels, Archangels, and Archai who help and guide them. They also seek a connection to Rudolf Steiner, to Michael, and to the Christ so that they can educate students in light of the spiritual and human needs of our time.

I hope that my thoughts in this essay will help those working in any Waldorf school to develop a deeper connection to the founding impulse of The Waldorf School. That impulse, as expressed through The Opening Address, The College Founding, and the preparatory course, gives us ever-renewing strength, courage, and wisdom for our daily tasks.

In this essay I have continually referred to the spiritual realm, but I have deliberately refrained from being too explicit because I do not consider myself qualified to do so. The

---

*Rudolf Steiner uses this term in a much broader way than it is typically intended in Christian church denominations. He speaks of the Christ as, among other things, the spiritual archetype of humanity's capacity for love. Readers should be aware that the author of this article is using the term in this sense.

spiritual realm is perceptible to spiritual organs which must be developed individually and can be nurtured collectively. The spiritual realm expresses itself in at least as many ways as the material realm, and it would be a disservice to share my own view as if it were somehow applicable to others.

The spiritual work of the College must be a practical endeavor in the sense that it must be practiced, but every group of people needs to work together to figure out how they wish to do it. None of us is qualified to do spiritual work; we qualify ourselves by our striving, and we should not hold back because we consider ourselves unworthy.

In his poem "Birches," Robert Frost describes a boy living far from town who climbs birch trees and swings himself back down to earth. When he feels that life is too much like a pathless wood, Frost says:

> I'd like to get away from earth awhile
> And then come back to it and begin over.
> May no fate willfully misunderstand me
> And half grant what I wish and snatch me away
> Not to return. Earth's the right place for love:
> I don't know where it's likely to go better.

Earth is the right place for love. It is the only place for love. As Rudolf Steiner said, "Human beings are born to have the possibility of doing what they cannot do in the spiritual world."[26] In the spiritual world we do not have the freedom that allows us to experience or express love; we need to be human beings to do so. As spiritual beings we come to earth, take on physical bodies, and live in the material realm because it is the right place for love. It is the place where, as a College, we can work together in love for the good of humanity and of the earth.

Appendix
The Opening Address, given on the eve of the Teachers' Seminar, Stuttgart, August 20, 1919:

This evening I wish to make some preliminary remarks. To achieve a renewal of modern spiritual life, the Waldorf School must be a true cultural deed. We must reckon with change in everything; the ultimate foundation of the whole social movement is in the spiritual realm and the question of education is one of the burning spiritual questions of modern times. We must take advantage of the possibilities presented by the Waldorf School to reform and revolutionize the educational system. The success of this cultural deed is in your hands. Thus, you have much responsibility in working to create an example. So much depends upon the success of this deed. The Waldorf School will be living proof of the effectiveness of the anthroposophical orientation toward life. It will be a unified school in the sense that it only considers how to teach in the way demanded by the human being, by the totality of the human essence. We must put everything at the service of achieving this goal.

However, it is necessary that we make compromises, because we are not yet so far developed that we can accomplish a truly free deed. The state imposes terrible learning goals and terrible standards, the worst imaginable, but people will imagine them to be the best. Today's policies and political activity treat people like pawns. More than ever before, attempts will be made to use people like cogs in a wheel. People will be handled like puppets on a string, and everyone will think that this reflects the greatest progress imaginable. Things like institutions of learning will be created incompetently and with the greatest arrogance. We have a foretaste of this in the design of the Russian Bolshevik schools, which are graves for everything that represents true teaching.

We have a difficult struggle ahead of us, but, nevertheless, we must do this cultural deed. We must bring two contradictory forces into harmony. On the one hand, we must know what our ideals are, and, on the other hand, we must have the flexibility to conform to what lies far from our ideals. It will be difficult for each of you to find how to bring these two forces into harmony. This will be possible to achieve only when each of you enters into this work with your full strength. Everyone must use his or her full strength from the very beginning.

Therefore, we will organize the school not bureaucratically, but collegially, and will administer it in a republican way. In a true teachers' republic we will not have the comfort of receiving directions from the Board of Education. Rather, we must bring to our work what gives each of us the possibility and the full responsibility for what we have to do. Each one of us must be completely responsible.

We can create a replacement for the supervision of the School Board as we form this preparatory course and, through the work, receive what unifies the school. We can achieve that sense of unity through this course if we work with all diligence. The course will be held as a continuing discussion of general pedagogical questions, as a discussion of the special methods concerning the most important areas of instruction, and as a seminar to practice teaching. We will practice teaching and critique it through discourse.

We will take up the more theoretical aspects in the morning and the seminar in the afternoon on each day. We will begin at 9:00am with general pedagogy, then undertake instruction concerning special methods at 11:30, and in the afternoon do seminar exercises from 3:00 until 6:00.

We must be completely conscious that we have to accomplish a great cultural deed in every sense of the word. Here in the Waldorf School we do not wish to create a parochial school. The Waldorf School will not propagate a particular point of view by filling the children with anthroposophical dogma. We do not wish to teach anthroposophical dogma; anthroposophy is not the content of the instruction. What we want is a practical utilization of anthroposophy. We want to transform what we can gain through anthroposophy into truly practical instruction.

The anthroposophical content of instruction is much less important than the practical utilization of what we can create out of anthroposophy, generally in pedagogy and particularly in the special methods; in other words, how we can bring anthroposophy into teaching practice.

Representatives of the confessions will give religious instruction. We will use anthroposophy only in the method of instruction. Therefore, we will divide the children among the religion teachers according to their confession. This is another part of the compromise. Through justifiable compromises we can accelerate our cultural deed.

We must be conscious of the great tasks before us. We dare not be simply educators; we must be people of culture in the highest sense of the word. We must have a living interest in everything happening today; otherwise we will be bad teachers for this school. We dare not have enthusiasm only for our special tasks. We can be good teachers only when we have a living interest in everything happening in the world. Through that interest in the world, we must obtain the enthusiasm that we need for the school and for our tasks. Flexibility of spirit and devotion to our tasks are necessary. Only from that can we draw out what can be achieved today when we devote our interest to the great needs and tasks of the times, both of which are unimaginably large.

The College Founding, given at the beginning of the Preparatory Course Stuttgart, August 21, 1919:

We can accomplish our work only if we do not see it as simply a matter of intellect or feeling, but, in the highest sense, as a moral spiritual task. Therefore, you will understand why, as we begin this work today, we first reflect on the connection we wish to create from the very beginning between our activity and the spiritual worlds. With such a task, we must be conscious that we do not work only in the physical plane of living human beings. In the last centuries, this way of viewing work has increasingly gained such acceptance that it is virtually the only way people see it. This understanding of tasks has made teaching what it is now and what the work before us should improve. Thus, we wish to begin our preparation by first reflecting upon how we connect with the spiritual powers in whose service and in whose name each one of us must work. I ask you to understand these introductory words as a kind of prayer to those powers who stand behind us with Imagination, Inspiration and Intuition as we take up this task.

[The words that follow were not recorded by the stenographer—see Herbert Hahn's notes below.]

It is our duty to see the importance of our work. We will do this if we know that this school is charged with a particular task. We need to make our thoughts very concrete; we need to form our thoughts so that we can be conscious that this school fulfills something special. We can do this only when we do not view the founding of this school as an everyday occurrence, but instead regard it as a ceremony held within Cosmic Order. In this sense, I wish, in the name of the good spirit whose task it is to lead humanity out of suffering and misery, in the name of this good spirit whose task it is to lead humanity to a higher level of development in education, I wish to give the most heartfelt thanks to this good spirit who has given our dear friend Mr. Molt the good thoughts to do what he has done for the further development of humanity at this time and in this place, and what he has done for the Waldorf School. I know that he is aware that what can be done in this work now can only be done with weakened strength. He sees things in this way. However, because we are united with him in feeling the greatness of the task and of the moment in which it is begun, and in feeling that this is a festive moment in Cosmic Order, he will be able to work in our midst with the necessary strength. We wish to begin our work with this in mind. We wish to see each other as human beings brought together by karma, who will bring about, not something common, but something that, for those doing this work, will include the feeling of a festive Cosmic moment. At the end of our course I will say what I would like to say following today's festive commencement of our preparation. Then much will have been clarified, and we will be able to stand before our task much more concretely than we can today.

Notes from Herbert Hahn:
In that we actively turn to the pedagogy of this fifth cultural epoch, and in that we wish to be active as teachers, we may carry in consciousness the fact that the Beings of the Third Hierarchy are now moving to connect themselves with our work.

Behind each individual member of the now-forming faculty, we see an Angel standing. He lays both hands upon the head of the earthly being entrusted to him, and in this position and with this gesture allows strength to flow over to the human. It is the strength that provides the Imaginations necessary for the deed to be completed. Creatively Imagining, wakening powerful Imaginations, the Angel thus stands behind each individual. Raising our view higher, we see hovering above the heads of this forming faculty a host of Archangels. Circling again and again, they carry from each of us to the other what results from our spiritual encounter with our own Angel. And they carry it, enriched by the strength of all the others, back to us. In this circle, which acts like an activity of spiritual formation, a vessel is formed above the heads of those united in this common striving. This vessel is formed from a specific substance—Courage. At the same time, these circling, connecting Archangels allow creatively Inspirational forces to enter into their movements. The Archangels open the source for those Inspirations necessary for our work. Raising our view still higher, it rises up to the realm of the Archai. They are not represented in their entirety. However, from their realm, the Realm of Light, they let a drop descend into the vessel of Courage. We feel that this drop of Light is given to us from the good Spirit of our Time, who stands behind the Founder and the Founding of this new school. It is the creative forces of Intuition at work in this drop of Light. The Archai want to awaken the necessary Intuition in those now entering this new pedagogical work. Giving Strength, Courage and Light, beings of the Third Hierarchy take part in what is now being founded. Imaginatively, Inspiringly, Intuitively, they wish to connect with our earthly deeds.

Endnotes

1. The "College of Teachers" is the English phrase for the German term *Lehrerkollegium*. I have preserved the capitalization as a way of honoring this group's identity. Throughout this article I will use the terms "College" and "College of Teachers" interchangeably in recognition of the fact that many Colleges include non-teaching members. In the coming years I hope another name will be found that more accurately expresses the unique nature and work of this group.

2. The German title *Allgemeine Menschenkunde* has been translated and published as *Study of Man* and more recently as *Foundations of Human Experience* (Great Barrington, MA: SteinerBooks, 1996).

3. The German term *Einheitschule* that Rudolf Steiner used in this context had a very specific meaning during the late 19th and early 20th centuries. In *Education and Society in Modern Germany* (Routledge, 2003) R.H. Samuel characterized the *Einheitschule*: "This term denoted coordination of all aspects of education into a unified whole, in such a way that elementary, intermediate and secondary schools would cease to be separate categories, diversely administered and with unrelated curricula, and become integral elements in a harmonious whole." The Waldorf School was non-traditional in many other respects; it was non-denominational, coeducational, and had a curriculum that combined elements of the classical and technical schools.

4. Christof Wiechert, "The Seven Virtues of the Art of Teaching," in *Education—Health for Life*, published by the Medical Section at the Goetheanum, Switzerland, 2006.

5. Rudolf Steiner, *Foundations of Human Experience*, p. 30.

6. Rudolf Steiner, *Towards Social Renewal* (London: Rudolf Steiner Press, 1977).

7. Rudolf Steiner, *Faculty Meetings with Rudolf Steiner* (Hudson, NY: Anthroposophic Press, 1998), pp. 154–155.

8. Rudolf Steiner, *Towards the Deepening of Waldorf Education* (Dornach: Pedagogical Section of the School of Spiritual Science, 1991), p. 83.

9. Rudolf Steiner, *Practical Advice to Teachers* (Great Barrington, MA: Anthroposophic Press, 2000), p. 189.

10. Rudolf Grosse, *The Christmas Foundation: Beginning of a New Cosmic Age* (Great Barrington, MA: SteinerBooks, 1984), p. 132.

11. Rudolf Steiner, *The Renewal of the Social Organism* (Hudson, NY: Anthroposophic Press, 1985).

12. "Brotherhood and the Fight for Survival," Berlin, November 23, 1905. Available online at http://wn.rsarchive.org/Lectures/19051123p01.html.

13. Ibid.

14. Rudolf Steiner, *Awakening to Community* (Spring Valley, NY: Anthroposophic Press, 1974), pp. 92–95.

15. Ibid., p. 156.

16. Ibid., p. 157.

17. Rudolf Steiner, *Foundations of Human Experience* (Hudson, NY: Anthroposophic Press, 1996), p. 33.

18. Ibid., p. 34.

19. *Towards the Deepening of Waldorf Education: Excerpts from the Work of Rudolf Steiner* (Dornach: Pedagogical Section of the School of Spiritual Science, 1991), p. 59.

20. Rudolf Steiner, *The Younger Generation* (Spring Valley, NY: Anthroposophic Press, 1976), p. 174.

21. Rudolf Steiner, *Deeper Insights into Waldorf Education* (Hudson, NY: Anthroposophic Press, 1988), pp. 50–51.

22. Rudolf Steiner, *Rudolf Steiner in the Waldorf School* (Hudson, NY: Anthroposophic Press, 1996), p. 59.

23. Ibid., p. 58.

24. Ibid., p. 62.

25. Ibid., p. 207.

26. Rudolf Steiner, *Foundations of Human Experience*, p. 44.

Contemplative Work in the College Meeting

Elan Leibner

Introduction

The possibility of developing a successful collaborative, spiritual-leadership model depends on the participants' ability to become, collectively, a vessel for wisdom greater than their own. This wisdom may reveal itself in fundamental insights (Moral Intuitions, in the language of *Intuitive Thinking as a Spiritual Path*[1]), creative visions for addressing the ramifications of those insights (Moral Imaginations), or plans for incarnating the visions into the specific reality in which the school is operating (Moral Technique). While individuals may well be capable of achieving some of those steps on their own, the fundamental idea of the collaborative model is that single capacities can be enhanced through collaboration. Furthermore, collaboration may indeed allow individual capacities to reach their full fruition by providing the listening attentiveness that often holds the key to sounding out one's inherent potential.

A second facet of this model is the spiritual dimension: The group is engaged with spiritual beings, and this engagement implies spiritual effort. This dimension is the one with which this essay is primarily concerned. The third facet is the element of leadership; the model is meant to offer guidance that can be followed by the school. Engaging in spiritual work, even in a collaborative fashion, is insufficient in itself; the group still needs to provide leadership. The guiding imagination for this model, at least in Waldorf schools, is the so-called College Imagination, delivered by Rudolf Steiner at the inception of the *Study of Man* course in 1919.[2]

Steiner describes a circle of teachers, with each member's Angel standing behind him/her, placing a hand on the teacher's head, and allowing strength to stream forth. Steiner later refers to this as "the spiritual meeting of each individual with his angel." This strength allows imaginations to stream into the pedagogical work. Above, Archangels are gathering the strength, which "has been enhanced through uniting with all the others," and make "a chalice of courage" out of it. Into this chalice, Archai (angelic beings of a higher order than the Archangels) allow a drop of light to fall. Light is a spiritual term synonymous with wisdom, and the process of helping teachers become recipients of light in the manner indicated by the College Imagination is the main subject of this essay.

Crucial for the idea we are trying to develop here is Steiner's description of how the capacity to receive intuitive wisdom ("drop of light") is preceded by the forming of a vessel ("chalice of courage"), and how this vessel is composed of "what is coming to birth through the spiritual meeting of each individual with his angel." It is clear that this *spiritual meeting* is the very foundation of the collaborative spiritual model being inaugurated. I would suggest that this meeting consists of inner, meditative work.

The space here is too limited for a full discussion of the nature of inner work, yet a few germane points can be singled out. One such point is what Steiner calls "the gate of humility."[3] When one practices humility in the pursuit of wisdom, an enhanced ability to relinquish a supposed ownership of ideas, or to allow better ideas to improve and/or change what had been brought into the discussion follows. The very notion of reaching for higher wisdom suggests that there exists a wisdom higher than what one may presently possess. Absent this practice, one may cling to one's "own" ideas out of an all-too-human vanity. But one learns on a meditative path to release one's attachment to ideas-as-possessions. Ideas are placed at the service of others, or, in this instance, of the leadership process. This is, I believe, what Steiner meant when he spoke of the Archangels carrying from one individual to the other "what is coming to birth through the spiritual meeting of each individual with his angel." I will refer to this later in this essay as "freed spiritual substance." It means ideas that have been freed from ownership. Together a group of such ideas can serve as the preparatory vessel, or chalice.

A second contribution of the inner path is the notion that one's colleague is also "on the path." Sensing that the other, too, is working to become a better vessel for the spirit increases the willingness to be patient with his or her idiosyncrasies, since there is hope that the gaps that yawn between colleagues may narrow in the next minute (or the next year). Colleagues are less likely to view each other as forever destined to remain the same. Sustained over years, colleagueship in Waldorf schools needs the optimism that the hope (indeed the anticipation) of change brings. Group processes can otherwise suffer "occlusions of the light" born of the blindness people always have for the "better angels of [each other's] nature." The willingness to see—and the practice of seeing—the good in one's colleagues forms an essential aspect of what Steiner calls the reverse ritual, meaning the elevation of the striving community to the company of spiritual beings.

The most important contribution that a meditative practice offers a collaborative spiritual-leadership model, however, is the presence of concentrated, receptive attentiveness. A meditative path begins with exercises to improve the focus of one's attention. Once attention is focused on a "something," we can remove that "something" and have a moment of becoming aware of attention itself as a form-free *capacity. Empty, receptive attention* is the pre-requisite for new ideas. When a group can develop an "empty attention," when it is available and willing to receive new ideas, it has also developed an essential aspect of the "chalice of courage." The surest way for developing this collective capacity is for the individual members to engage in developing their own capacities.

We can say, therefore, that for this collaborative spiritual-leadership model to succeed, the members of the leadership group should be actively engaged in a meditative practice. It is indeed my view that most of the failings of Colleges of Teachers in Waldorf schools can be traced to the absence of sufficient meditative work. Freed spiritual substance (created and freed through the individuals' meditative efforts) is then missing for the chalice-forming activity of benevolent spiritual beings, and the members of the College are left with nothing but their too-limited earthly powers. "Drops of light" can be difficult to receive without the spiritual chalice having been formed. Even when individual members receive new ideas, the receptivity of the group is not sufficient for these ideas to become fruitful.

Assuming that the collaborative-leadership model depends on individual meditative practice, a new difficulty arises. An individual inner path is difficult to establish. During teacher-preparation courses, many a student focuses on other aspects of the profession, and the habit life of a meditative practice is not firmly established. Afterwards, many new teachers make an attempt, encounter the inevitable obstacles, and essentially give up on a regular practice, perhaps replacing a cognitive path with prayer. Such individuals may even be quite gifted teachers, but their capacity to serve as contributors in a chalice-forming process is undoubtedly compromised. Sooner or later they come up against obstacles (some alluded to here, others elsewhere in this publication) and, absent the tools developed through inner practice, they may either burn out or burn others out. Burnout is essentially the consequence of an inability to renew oneself, and renewal, in this context, means tapping the source of new ideas.

Sometimes a school will have a few "old timers" who have an active meditative life that allows them to carry the spiritual essence of Waldorf education and serve as pillars for the work of the College. But as they begin to retire or move on to other chapters in their biographies, a kind of spiritual implosion results. Colleagues, parents, and former students may remark that the school "doesn't feel the same anymore." Whereas the implied change is not necessarily bad, it may point to a kind of active absence, if you will, of that "something" that made the school work more deeply in the past. Peripheral teachers are asked to become central pillars and leaders of chalice-forming practices, yet they lack the foundation of an independent spiritual practice. This possible picture is not to suggest that every old-timer is a meditative practitioner, or that newer colleagues are not meditants, but merely to point towards a phenomenon that may illustrate the role of meditative practice in the collaborative spiritual-leadership model.

If we agree that contemplative practice is crucial to successful leadership in Waldorf schools, and that establishing this practice is fraught with challenges, are there steps that can be taken to support individual teachers attempting to develop such a practice? Practicing exercises and even engaging in contemplative work in groups can be of great help for those trying to launch an individual meditative life. The reason might be that successful concentration is often easier to achieve when undertaken with others. Whereas as physical organisms we are always separated from one another, in soul and spirit we are more woven together; the efforts of those around us can help draw our spiritual capacities in the desired direction. There are legitimate concerns about doing this work in groups, and some of those concerns will be addressed below, but once individuals experience what a concentrated state "feels like," they are more likely to persevere in attempting to reach it on their own. Put another way, once we know what we are looking for, we may have more patience trying to find it. Even for people with many years of faithful practice, doing contemplative work together can provide enhanced strength, often leading to new and surprising directions in their individual work. Hearing how others have approached a verse or an image is helpful when the sharing is done with the proper restraint, but actually practicing *that* approach with them seems to offer a gift, a benefit born of their many years of practice. One feels "gifted" by one's colleague, and deeply thankful.

In my own experience, a College that had struggled for years to overcome personality-driven conflicts and endless debate was transformed within a matter of weeks into a far more receptive and cogent leadership group once various forms of inner work were practiced during the opening segment of meetings. In my view this occurred because the shared substance of the opening segment was already uniting the individuals' higher capacities by the time discussion of school matters began. The College members had engaged a demanding text or an exercise, had spent time reflecting on the content or the experience, and had dedicated themselves and their efforts toward the wellbeing of the school. A shift had occurred in their consciousness and mood. The daily hubbub of teaching and the experience of interacting with people on the level of intellectual, informational consciousness had been replaced by a period of intentional dedication at the contemplative level. The ground was then prepared for a different kind of interaction.

It might be argued that shared substance can also be created through ordinary study. The essential difference, however, is that in contemplative work the shared substance is actively taken into each individual's inner life, and the attempt is made to understand the "content" at the level from which it originated. Rudolf Steiner (or another spiritual researcher) had experiences across the threshold, and then had to "clothe" those in words; our task as students is to proceed in the reverse direction, starting from the words and reaching across the threshold to the experience. A conscious effort is undertaken as well to invite something more than one's ordinary understanding to enter the process, something that transcends what the individual is already thinking. In some "regular" studies, the discussion rarely, if ever, transcends the informational, content level. This informational level of consciousness is the level of arguments, not the level of humble receptivity indicated by the chalice imagination. But a group of people that has engaged in a period of contemplative practice is primed for a meeting that can become something more than "just a meeting." We can get a feeling for the difference from a lecture Steiner gave on February 28, 1923:

> And if several people come together with what they have
> from their everyday consciousness, and don't with full
> sensitivity lift themselves up to the supersensible world, if
> such people meet together merely to hear the language of
> the supersensible world in the everyday state of soul, then
> there is an infinitely great possibility that they may begin to
> argue, because in the most natural way they become egotists
> in relation to each other. ...If people take their normal soul
> life into their supposed understanding of the teaching from
> higher worlds, then of course this leads to egotism and
> argument.[4]

Objections and Dangers

Some people might object to the idea of contemplative work in groups because "Rudolf Steiner did not do this kind of work in groups, and therefore it is not appropriate for us to do it." This kind of orthodoxy is dangerous, since it restricts anthroposophy to precedent rather than allowing it to meet the moment, but it also misses an important factor: the effect of Rudolf Steiner's personal presence at the first Waldorf school. Anyone who has worked with a genuine spiritual researcher (e.g., Jørgen Smit or Georg Kühlewind) knows that listening to such a person is in itself a meditative exercise. His thoughts blaze a trail of light that has to be followed by attentiveness unlike the one we use for ordinary intellectual content. In *How to Know Higher Worlds* Steiner says of the communications of the spiritual researcher:

> For such instructions are culled from the living inner word...they are themselves gifted with spiritual life. They are not mere words; they are living powers. And while you follow the words of one who knows...powers are at work in your soul which make you clairvoyant.[5]

When Steiner assembled the first Waldorf school teachers and instructed them, the "content" was given in the *Study of Man* lectures and other such pearls of higher knowledge. When he attended their faculty meetings, the discussion was sometimes entirely practical, but then would veer into insights that could not be properly received without subsequent meditative reflection. Steiner assumed that the teachers were meditants, and he gave them "content" and even mantras to support their work. He spoke directly about the need to meditate on the "content" of his lectures:

And it is especially interesting to allow everything I have presented today to work on you; let it invigorate you. ... If you bring all these things together and form mental images of them in *active meditation*, you can be sure that the vigorous power of ingenuity you need when facing the children you are educating will be kindled in you.[6] [Emphasis mine]

In the absence of a spiritual researcher to guide the teachers in a school, other forms of support for the faculty members' meditative work may well be needed, and the exercises discussed here could be one approach for providing such support.

Contemplative work in groups does present some legitimate dangers, however. Those dangers are born of the temptations that beset the path toward higher knowledge, and just as the presence of others may help along this path, it can also exacerbate some of the pitfalls. A few of the potential dangers are discussed below, and a group that intends to pursue this kind of work is encouraged to discuss these and reach a set of agreements to mitigate them. This set of agreements may be spoken at the beginning of each session or in some form be mentioned as a reminder to those present.

Danger: Contemplative work in a group infringes on individual freedom by coercing a person to engage in it when s/he might not want or feel able to do so. Such a person would either engage in the practice against his/her better judgment, or, if the practice is expected of everyone, leave the group altogether. One possible solution is to engage in this work before the official beginning of the meeting; another option is to allow members to excuse themselves; a third possibility is to allow members to be present quietly without engaging in the work. Each group should decide how to handle this difficulty.

Danger: Since work in groups is easier for some, individuals might choose to replace their personal practice with group work. This is not what anthroposophy should promote. Anthroposophy is an individual spiritual path first and foremost. The group should discuss what, if anything, the members might commit to doing outside the meeting. In my view, some form of commitment to individual practice should become one of the agreements.

Danger: Individuals sometimes suggest or imply that they have achieved more in their practice (or during the group exercises) than is actually the case. This brings an element of untruth into the very heart of the school and creates a mood around the spiritual practice that is harmful rather than helpful. Absolute honesty, integrity, and humility must pervade every aspect of this work. Of course, these attributes are generally expected of College members, but a special emphasis should be placed on them in this context.

Danger: Details of people's individual spiritual life might be shared during parts of these sessions, leaving those individuals open to a breach of trust. Thus what was offered in full confidence can end up coming back in a completely different context. If the group discusses the question of moral character (see below), then additional aspects of vulnerability are placed in trust. Some form of agreement regarding confidentiality is needed. This might include provisions regarding (not) sharing with members absent from the group, and of course (not) sharing with non-members, including spouses. It cannot be overemphasized how important this agreement is for the long-term health of the group.

If these four dangers, in whichever form College members opt to address them, are countered, then I believe the group may safely engage in contemplative work together. As already mentioned, it is a good idea to have a short reminder of these agreements at the beginning of each session. Obviously, in specific circumstances additional agreements may be necessary, and every group is free to create and amend any agreements it makes.

Examples of Formats and Practices

A group will usually assign an individual to prepare and lead the sessions. This assignment may last for just one meeting or for an extended period of time. The group has to determine the scope of the leader's mandate in terms of choosing the themes and formats of the sessions. Some experimentation is recommended so that the comfort zone of a particular group can be established. Some groups need parameters set in advance (e.g., length of time for each session, length of assignment of leading the sessions, restrictions on the themes for meditation, and review format), while for other groups a more open-ended beginning is preferred. Even in open-ended beginnings, a review of the practice should be planned within the next two or three months, if not sooner. Inner work is delicate, and we do not want members of the group to have growing frustrations or resentments over issues that could be resolved through a review. A sensitive leader will seek to navigate the practice so that individual concerns may be addressed before they become festering problems, but a regular review is also important.

There are many ways to engage with contemplative content, of course. For the purpose of the work discussed here, three steps seem basic enough to be regarded as fundamental:

1. Centering: concentration exercise/s to focus the attention
2. Engagement (with the theme)
3. Review

There are other steps that could be considered. It is possible to begin a session with a dedication. The members dedicate the work to the school/organization and renounce personal gain or attachments. Another step that can have a profound effect is "stooping through the gate of humility." Members remind themselves of their own shortcomings and of the notion of a wisdom higher than one's own. By remembering Steiner's exhortation to take three steps in the perfection of one's moral character for every step taken in spiritual development, participants can think of three moments in the past day/week/month during which they fell short of their moral ideals. One then resolves to place three balancing gestures into the world during the following day.

However the session is opened, the first step in the actual work is centering. There are many examples of concentration exercises in the anthroposophical literature. Of particular note for all three of the steps mentioned above is Georg Kühlewind's little booklet, *The Light of the "I."* [7] It contains a wealth of practical guidance and examples of exercises, as well as advice on dealing with obstacles. The period of concentration cannot be too long because of time constraints, but it should not be shorter than a minute. A two- to five-minute timeframe is usually sufficient. Members may concentrate on a simple man-made object, the movement of the second-hand of a clock, or other non-interesting subject. The point is that the attention is focused through one's effort and not through the object's being interesting.

The second, central part of the session is engagement with the theme. This theme may be a verse (such as one of the Teachers Meditations), an image (such as Michael and the Dragon, or the *Rose Cross*), a theme from a lecture (such as the physiological locations of auditory and visual processes described in the third lecture of *Balance in Teaching*), or a phrase (such as "Wisdom lives in the Light"). The leader suggests a manner of working with the theme for that session, and the group engages. One example of working with a theme is to "condense the verse" into its verbs only, so that the meaning is sought through the movement of the verbs. If that is successful, the verbs, too, can be removed and the whole theme is held in wordless attentiveness. As with all meditations, the theme itself has to be removed after it is beheld wordlessly. Most people are not able to have an empty attentiveness for more than a brief moment, so one returns to the theme, reduces it, and tries to reach the empty state again. It is important that one is not worried about "getting somewhere" during this period, but simply engages as far as is possible on that day.

Another possibility is to imagine that one is writing the verse: Each word is "selected" from amongst other words in the "meaning vicinity" so that this word is chosen as opposed to that one. Thus "*Spirit* beholding" at the beginning of the second Teachers Meditation is chosen instead of "*soul*" or "*inward* beholding." Next, "*beholding*" is chosen instead of "*meditating*," or "*remembering*," and so on. The experience of "writing" the verse in this way gives one an intense level of identification with the text, much as one would have when writing a poem. One can contemplate a line, a section or an entire verse in this manner. Again, once the meaning has been explored, a wordless beholding should follow, and finally a removal of the theme itself.

There are many possibilities of working with themes, and the two chosen above should be taken only as examples to illustrate the process. Steiner's books, as well as those of other anthroposophical authors, offer an abundance of themes and instructions. In addition to the Kühlewind book mentioned earlier, Dennis Klocek and Jørgen Smit have also published excellent instructions. It is left for each group to determine, or leave it to the leader to determine, how long the engagement should last. A general suggestion is ten to fifteen minutes.

When the engagement period is over, some review should occur. The review can be brief or prolonged, done inwardly by each member or through a verbal exchange, but it should happen. It allows each member to re-cognize what just transpired and to thank the spiritual world for its help. If the review is conducted through conversation, the tone should be restrained and reverent. Questions, insights, and suggestions may be shared, but the conversation should not lapse into casual chitchat. There should also be a clear ending for this part of the meeting. The session leader or the meeting chair should clearly separate the meditative segment from the rest of the meeting. It may even be good to stand and stretch, or read a verse, in order to transition out of one mode of conversation and into another.

Concluding Thoughts

Waldorf education is nearing the hundred-year anniversary of its founding. In some respects, it is a mature movement with traditions, standards, and habits. In its essence, however, it is meant to be ever the newborn creation, mediating the intentions of spiritual beings directly into the physical world. I believe that the sine-qua-non of Waldorf education is the teachers' meditative lives. Unless a conscious path is cultivated for spiritual beings to support the human being, "Waldorf" will become ever more a noun, a thing. It is a bit better when used as an adjective, but perhaps we should aim to make it into a verb. We should aim "to Waldorf," meaning to actively connect a child to his/her pre-birth intentions, to work in such a way that our work is "a continuation of what higher beings have done before his birth" (*Study of Man*, Lecture 1). I hope that the path offered in this essay can be support for this intention.

Endnotes

1. Rudolf Steiner, *Intuitive Thinking as a Spiritual Path* (Hudson, NY: Anthroposophic Press, 1995).
2. Rudolf Steiner, *Study of Man* (Forest Row, Sussex, UK: Rudolf Steiner Press, 2007).
3. Rudolf Steiner, *How to Know Higher Worlds* (Hudson, NY: Anthroposophic Press, 1994).
4. Rudolf Steiner, *Awakening to Community* (Hudson, NY: Anthroposophic Press, 1974).
5. See note 3 above.
6. Rudolf Steiner, *Balance in Teaching*, Lecture 3 (Great Barrington, MA: Anthroposophic Press, 2007).
7. Georg Kühlewind, *The Light of the "I"* (Great Barrington, MA: Anthroposophic Press, 2008).

An Essential Teacher Meditation

Jane Wulsin

When Rudolf Steiner met with the twelve original Waldorf teachers on September 9, 1919, he gave them a meditative practice which is relatively simple in its form and absolutely essential for our work as Waldorf teachers. It was the means by which they could connect themselves every day to the Beings of the Third Hierarchy.

In the first meeting for the founding of the first Waldorf school, Rudolf Steiner addressed the teachers,

> Dear friends, we will do justice to our task only if we orient our consciousness in such a way that we take the spiritual world seriously. We may no longer live only within the material world. We must actually live together with the spiritual world. We must establish the link with the spiritual powers, on whose behalf and on whose mandate each one of us will have to work.

He told the teachers, "The Waldorf school would be an actual cultural deed to achieve renewal of spiritual life in the present." He said the teachers could feel themselves to be united with the will of the spiritual world, that they could become "self–aware tools in the service of the high spiritual powers who want to work through us."

In this vein, Rudolf Steiner spoke about how a Waldorf teacher needs to form a relationship to the Beings of the Third Hierarchy, similar to the relationship he tries to cultivate with the mineral kingdom before teaching geology, or to the plant kingdom before teaching botany. Far more difficult, however, it is to develop a relationship with angels, archangels, and archai than it is to make relationships within the natural world around us. One way of forging this connection, and at the same time of receiving help from them in carrying out our tasks, is to remember these beings consciously at two moments during the day.

The Third Hierarchy is the hierarchy which is closest and most accessible to the human being. These beings are particularly interested in the earth and human evolution, and they receive sustenance from human beings. The *angels* have a special relationship to our thoughts, particularly to our ideals. Through our astral body, feeling flows into our words. The *archangels* are nourished by the idealism and purity of feeling present in our language. Our "I" is connected to the movement of our limbs. The *archai* have an intimate relationship to our will life, especially when it reveals a genuine interest in and love for others. Each night when we go to sleep, these beings are waiting to see what ideals we bring with us into the spiritual world. They are nourished by our striving and by our interest in and love for every human being.

We are also reminded of the special tasks which the Third Hierarchy has within the first three seven-year periods. During the first twenty-one years of life, the activity of soul and spirit works to develop all aspects of the individuality, and the angels, archangels, and archai work strongly upon this soul-spiritual substance. Whereas they are focusing their efforts on the developing child particularly during these first three seven-year periods, their influence on our soul life continues throughout life.

The activity of the Third Hierarchy is, therefore, an intricate part of our lives, of the children's lives, and of our work. These beings are connected to the soul forces thinking, feeling, and willing; they are working actively in the development of the child and young person; they have a particular relationship to the renewal of culture through Waldorf education. Our task as Waldorf teachers is to form a close and more active relationship with them so that the children and, ultimately, the Earth's evolution, may benefit from a more conscious working together.

Rudolf Steiner suggested a way to do this. "In the evening, before meditation, ask the angels, the archangels, and the archai to help in your work the following day." This is an active cosmic communion, reaching out to the Beings of the Third Hierarchy and asking them to participate in our work. This type of meditation is known as the chalice ritual or "the reverse cultus." It is a way for the human being to lift himself into the supersensible world so that he may come to communion with spiritual beings.

Each day we do our preparation for the next day. We may be well-prepared or under-prepared. We have certainly never penetrated the material with the task to the degree we would have liked. We hope that we have done the best we could, given our particular circumstances; we take our efforts and offer them up to the spiritual world. This is our offering, however meager, and we ask that it be fructified by the beings with whom we hope to work. Johannes Tautz gives the image of opening oneself and of beseechingly lifting up the chalice. It is we who are standing at the altar, and we are offering ourselves, our own substance.[1]

During the night, the four members of our being are interpenetrated by the beings of hierarchies. A spiritual communion occurs. Our efforts are received, and they are fructified by spiritual substance. In the morning what we have offered has been changed. We have received a gift of spiritual substance. Rudolf Steiner asks that, after a meditation, we have the thought and feeling: "You beings, with whom I was united during the night, help me in what I do today. I am under your care; I want to be your self-aware instrument. I know the Beings of the Third Hierarchy will be with me in my work."

Through this meditative activity we connect ourselves consciously with the angels, archangels, and archai. We open ourselves to their influence and ask that they participate in our work. When we are in the classroom with the children, we know we are not alone. Indeed, we know we cannot possibly accomplish tasks by ourselves. This connecting ourselves to the Beings of the Third Hierarchy, through our heart-felt striving, enables us to have the right imagination, inspiration, or intuition in the moment. We will be more likely able to do or say what is needed in the moment for the situation which presents itself. In the preparation of our lessons, we will also be better able to separate the essential from the non-essential and to find what we need for our class or for a particular child.

This meditation takes relatively little effort, except for the huge effort of remembering to do it, but it is a necessity for work. We have the choice of stumbling rather blindly through our classes by ourselves or of trying to work more consciously with those mighty spiritual beings who want to co-create with us and who can help us truly become Waldorf teachers for our amazing, deserving students.

Endnote
1. Tautz, Johannes, *The Founding of the First Waldorf School in Stuttgart*, Ghent, NY: AWSNA Publications, 2011, p. 43.

The Artistic Meeting: Creating Space for Spirit

Holly Koteen-Soulé

When Rudolf Steiner brought together the individuals who would become the teachers of the first Waldorf school, he asked them to work in a new way, not only with the children, but also with one another. He asked them to work together in such as way as to invite the interest and guidance of spiritual beings into their endeavor.

The challenge of creating and maintaining a connection with the spiritual world, as difficult as it was then, may be even more intense in the present time. Materialism has grown considerably stronger in the 21st century, and with it has come an increasing need to bring a balancing, healing, and renewing element to daily life.

The Waldorf classroom is a place where this renewing spiritual element can be found. It arises from the children themselves and from how we work with them. It can also be found in the meeting life of the school, in how the teachers and other adults work together. There are many resources available today on how to conduct effective meetings in the workplace. This article will focus on how we can create a space for spirit in meetings and how this endeavor can support us in our individual development, in our encounters with colleagues, and in strengthening our groups and communities.

Meetings as an artistic activity will be a second focus. Understanding meetings as an art form and using an artistic approach when planning and carrying out a meeting can allow participants to be refreshed and inspired at the meeting's conclusion. While including an artistic activity in the agenda can be helpful, it is more critical that the meeting itself be artistic and display the wholeness, drama, and dynamics of any other artistic creation. Artistic activity can often be a doorway to the recognition of spiritual archetypes and the building of spiritual understanding. A meeting that is conducted as a form of art greatly enhances this possibility for the participants.

MEETINGS AS SPIRITUAL PRACTICE

Waking up in the Other

Near the end of his life, after the burning of the first Goetheanum and during a period of upheaval within the Anthroposophical Society, Rudolf Steiner began to speak urgently about the need to build communities based on a shared spiritual purpose that extends beyond our cultural or hereditary ties. He described physical waking as a response to the stimuli of the natural world in our surroundings. Our waking up at a higher level happens when we encounter the soul-spirit of other human beings. He went so far as to say:

> We are also unable to understand the spiritual world, no matter how many beautiful ideas we may have garnered from anthroposophy or how much we may have grasped theoretically about such matters as etheric and astral bodies. We begin to develop an understanding for the spiritual world only when we wake up in the encounter with the soul-spiritual in our fellow men.[1]

On other occasions, Steiner also spoke about a need in our age (the 5th Post-Atlantean epoch) that can be fulfilled only in groups. He referred specifically to the spirit of brother/sisterhood hovering above us in the realm of the higher hierarchies, which needs to be consciously cultivated so that it can flow into human souls in the future. These statements constitute a strong call for us to create opportunities for more, rather than fewer, encounters with our colleagues, despite the inevitable challenges with which we are all familiar.

The Reverse Ritual

In considering meetings as spiritual practice, it may be helpful to recall our understanding from anthroposophy that at a certain point in the course of the evolution of the cosmos and humanity, the higher creative beings drew back from the sphere of the earth. This withdrawal was necessary in order for human beings to develop in freedom. As a result, the physical earth is in the process of dying. The human being, having been given freedom and the possibility of spiritual consciousness, has become an increasingly decisive factor in the future of the earth.

One of our tasks is to help re-enliven the earth. We do that with the substance of our human thinking—not our ordinary thoughts and reflections, but spiritual thoughts arising from creative Imaginations, Inspirations, and Intuitions. For Steiner these creative thoughts represented a new spiritual form of communion for humanity. He gave many indications about how both individuals and groups could work with creative, enlivening thoughts for their own benefit and for the benefit of humanity as a whole.

It was Steiner's deep conviction that the appropriate form for community-building in our time is what he called the reverse ritual. He distinguished this ritual from a traditional religious ritual, in which a mediator is charged with drawing the spiritual hierarchies down to a particular place. "The anthroposophical community seeks to lift up the human souls into supersensible worlds so that they may enter into the company of angels."

We must do more than talk about spiritual beings; we must look for opportunities nearest at hand to enter their company. The work of an anthroposophical group does not consist in a number of people merely discussing anthroposophical ideas. Its members should feel so linked with one another that human soul wakes up in the encounter with human soul and all are lifted up into the spiritual world, into the company of spiritual beings, though it need not be a question of beholding them. We do not have to see them to have this experience. [2]

The College Imagination (also known as the Teachers Imagination) that Steiner gave to the first group of teachers is an example of such a reverse ritual, in which a group working with a common meditative picture creates the possibility of connecting with specific spiritual beings and bringing back creative impulses for their earthly work.[3]

If Waldorf teachers wish to work with these ideas and with the example of the Teachers Imagination, how can we form and conduct faculty and college meetings in this light? How can our meeting life be spiritually sustaining for individuals and build a vital sense of community in our schools?

Space for Spirit

We know what it feels like to have participated in a successful meeting. We are enlivened at the meeting's end. We also know that what occurred could not have been achieved by any individual member of the group. These are indicators of spirit presence. It is possible to learn how to create such meetings—meetings that lift us out of our ordinary awareness and allow us the possibility of working more consciously with the spiritual world. We can create more space for spirit in our meeting life in the following ways.

I. *Imbue the meeting place with a sense of conscious care.* It is often the case that certain individuals have a natural feeling for the need to prepare the room where a meeting will occur. When we prepare a space with care, we are working with the elementals, spiritual beings which, according to Rudolf Steiner, are detachments from the higher hierarchies, sacrificing themselves for the creation of the material world. They have a great deal to do with the physical setting, and also with our individual physical well-being, our thinking, feeling, and willing, and our communications.

In my own experience, how the room is prepared can have as significant an effect on a meeting as it does on what happens in our classrooms when we make sure that they are clean, orderly, and beautiful. Imagine how the arrangement of the furniture could enhance the quality of the group's interaction. Consider the effect of having as a centerpiece a seasonal bouquet gathered by a member of the group, rather than one that was purchased at the florist shop. It is especially helpful if all members of a faculty take turns at preparing the setting, so that more members of the group carry the importance of this aspect of the meeting.

II. *Create a threshold mood.* Meetings that begin with a moment of silence and a mood of reverence allow participants to be aware of stepping across a kind of threshold, out of their everyday consciousness into a heightened sense of presence. An explicit acknowledgment of our spiritual helpers, the spirit of the school, and those persons who have been connected to our institution and are now in the spiritual world can also shift the group's awareness. A conscious effort to begin on time helps create the sense of going through a doorway together. A verse can also represent a threshold and, when brought in the right mood, offer a kind of protective sheath for whatever may happen in the meeting.

III. *Re-establish the sense of the group.* This activity has two parts. The first is the recognition of individuals, and the second is an affirmation of the purpose of the group. A key to the first part is the interest that we take in one another. Listening to colleagues share something out of their lives or an aspect of their work with students can wake us up to one another in a potent way. The sharing can be brief and, in the case of a large faculty, may involve only a portion of the group each week. Sharing can also be connected to the season; for example, at Michaelmas the focus could be: "What in your life is requiring a fresh burst of courage and will?"

This part of the meeting can deepen our understanding of our colleagues and build the level of trust that we need to work together on spiritual matters. Movement or artistic activity can also serve to strengthen the group's capacity to work together on issues that require sensitivity to one another. At this stage of the meeting, the "I" of each individual is acknowledged as he or she steps into the work with the group, or the "We."

The second part of establishing the sense of the group requires an affirmation of the group's purpose or task. A verse or reading can be helpful but must be relevant and alive for the group. For some groups, it may be important to choose a new opening for each year or to work with festival themes in order to strengthen the sense of community and purpose at this stage of the meeting. For other groups, choosing to work consciously with the same verse for many years may actually bring them to an ever-deepening understanding of its meaning and effect. While study is often used to bring a group to a common focus, this is successful only if everyone is actively engaged.

IV. *Practice conscious listening and speaking.* We know that listening perceptively to another person requires letting go of our sympathies and antipathies and our own preconceived ideas; in fact, we must momentarily let go of our own "I" to experience the "I" of the other as he or she speaks. Marjorie Spock wrote most poetically about the effects of perceptive listening:

First, there is what it does to the soul of the listener. A miracle of self-overcoming takes place within him whenever he really lends an ear to others. If he is to understand the person speaking, he must draw his attention from his own concerns and make a present of it to a listener; he clears his inner scene like one who for a time gives up his home for others' use while himself remaining only in the role of servant. Listeners quite literally entertain a speaker's thought. "Not I, but the Christ in me" is made real in every such act of genuine listening.

Second, there is what happens to the speaker when he is fortunate to be listened to perceptively. Another kind of miracle takes place in him, perhaps best described as a springtime burgeoning. Before his idea was expressed to a listener, it lived in his soul as potential only; it resembles a seed force lying fallow in the winter earth. To be listened to with real interest acts upon this seed like sun and warmth and rain and other cosmic elements that provide growth-impetus; the soul ground in which the idea is embedded comes magically alive. Under such benign influence, thoughts grow full cycle and fulfill their promise. Moreover, they confer fertility upon the ground through the simple fact of having lived there. Further ideas will be the more readily received into such a soil and spring more vigorously for its life-attunement. And the soul that harbors them begins to be the creative force in evolution for which it was intended by the gods.[4]

Brief spaces of silence can also allow thoughts and insights to ripen and fall into the conversation. Can we provide for the seed thoughts of our colleagues, out of our own souls, what the sun and rain provide for the sprouting plant? It is a rare group that does not need to recommit regularly to practicing this kind of listening and speaking.

V. *Work with imaginative pictures over time.* Imagination is a language that can bear fruit in the spiritual world. Translating the group's questions and issues into stories and pictures can enhance the group's meditative work during the meeting and individual work during the course of the week. Look for an archetype, myth, or fairy tale that can reveal new aspects of the matter under consideration. Taking time over two or three meetings to explore major questions invites the possibility of richer insights. Colleagues will want to hold back from building support for one or another course of action and to be open to new information as it emerges during this phase. Having worked successfully with imaginative pictures in the child study process can help build trust in their use in other situations as well.

VI. *Share responsibility.* Individuals who are able to carry the consciousness for a group have certain capacities that are usually recognized by the other members of the group. Not everyone has these in the same measure, but it is important to recognize talents among colleagues and give one another opportunities and support to develop latent capacities. Different individuals can lead various parts of a meeting. A group of two or three people can plan the agenda. Incorporate means of regular review for those taking responsibility for the yearly schedule.

It is clear that a group is healthiest when individuals are continuing to grow and develop. Even the most competent facilitator needs to step back or work with a new colleague in order to gain fresh perspective. Rotating leadership and having several individuals carry one or another aspect of the meeting facilitation make it more likely that all members will feel involved. All members are responsible to bring to the group the results of their individual meditative life. Spiritual leadership requires learning how to create the conditions for meaningful conversations and then helping the group follow up on what arises out of those conversations.

VII. *Let the meeting breathe.* In the work of the classroom we need to prepare carefully and be ready to respond to what comes from our students. A meeting that has a compelling wholeness and feeling of flow is probably the result of a well-crafted agenda along with some adjustments made during the meeting to an emerging sense of clarity and direction. Having prior agreements about how to deal with new information or agenda changes is helpful. A rhythmic relation to time in a meeting creates more of an opening for spiritual insights than either an overstuffed agenda or a formless one.

There are a number of simple possibilities for making a meeting more rhythmic. For example, honor the times on the agenda, but not so rigidly that people feel cut off or topics are truncated. Vary the conversation from full-group sharing to small-group work and individual reports. Create a balance between pedagogical and other topics, looking back and looking ahead, exploring new questions and making decisions. When the group is not moving physically, make sure there is plenty of inner movement. Remember to invite the spirit of Play and the spirit of Humor into the meeting.

VIII. *Expect to be surprised.* There is nothing more uninviting than a completely predictable meeting. On the other hand, a meeting in which the group is pulled this way and that by personal agendas is equally frustrating. We must stay awake to the influences of Ahriman (too much form) and Lucifer (too much impulsiveness) as they work in individuals and in our groups.

In order to stay the course in the creative spiritual stream, we need to ask real questions, practice positivity and open-mindedness, be comfortable with not knowing, and expect answers and solutions to come from unexpected places.

IX. *Review.* During meeting review, we reflect on what went well and what could have been better, so that we can improve our work together. Review serves another important purpose as well. Just as our nightly review is a conversation-starter for the work with our own angel during sleep, our meeting review serves as a seed for the continuing conversation with the spiritual world between meetings.

Running late in a meeting is sometimes the reason that groups neglect review, but review can often capture essential aspects of a meeting in a brief and economical way. In this regard, poetry is more useful than prose. Brief characterizations, even one-word or one-image offerings, can illuminate hidden gems. Hearing individual voices during the review can be a supportive bookend to the work, like the personal sharing is at the beginning of a meeting.

Review is not a rehashing of any part of the meeting. It should bring to light aspects of content, processes, and interactions that can benefit from greater awareness on the part of individuals and the group. A perceptive facilitator will vary the means of review and offer questions to elicit information that might not otherwise be brought to light. "Where did we experience gratitude in the meeting?" "Were there any moments of unresolved tension?" "What did we do that might be of interest to our spiritual helpers?" Review in the form of an earnest question is the best kind of invitation to spirit beings.

X. *Prepare and follow up.* If we recognize that our meetings are a kind of ritual, then preparation and follow-up are as important as the meeting itself. Preparation requires more than a quick glance at a copy of the agenda. When individuals come to a meeting having thought about the issues and their colleagues the night before, the spiritual ground has already been tilled.

How we carry the questions as well as the tasks from one meeting to the next can make a difference in whether the seeds sowed will sprout healthily in the coming weeks. How each individual carries the group in between meetings will also make a difference. Working rhythmically with time has both a physical and a spiritual aspect. When we consciously release into the spiritual world ideas that have arisen in the group, it is possible that they will return in a more complete or archetypal form.

These are some of the realities that we may wish to take into consideration as we build a vessel for the spiritual aspect of our work, just as we pay attention to earthly realities in constructing a physical home for our schools.

MEETINGS AS ART

The Artistic Process

The arts, according to Rudolf Steiner, were experienced in earlier civilizations as more integral to life than is the case today. Artistic creativity, he said, was experienced as a transcendent spiritual activity, flowing out of the "spirit-attuned state" in which the human being lived in those times. Only since the rise of materialism has the status of art changed from necessity to luxury.[5]

Rudolf Steiner also observed that in our era a longing for the arts comes out of the recognition of the limits of abstract thinking. Ideas alone are not able to illuminate the world in its full richness; they can only point the way to a deeper reality. Artistic feeling, Steiner said, arises when we sense the presence of something mysterious, such as certain secrets of nature, which can only be revealed through our feeling. Knowing is a matter for the heart as well as the head. To discover a whole, living reality, we need to create, to practice art. He saw the fructification of the arts in our time as an important task for anthroposophy, and he took up various artistic projects himself during the latter part of his life.[6]

The present-day artist engaged in the creative process moves back and forth between sense perceptions and intuitive visions—awake, but in a somewhat dreamlike, feeling state. Steiner described the subtle changes that occur in a person engaged in aesthetic activity (regardless of whether the person is creating or enjoying an artistic creation) such that the sense organs are re-enlivened and the bodily life processes are lifted to soul-like processes.[7]

In artistic activity we use our heightened sense of feeling rather than our everyday sympathies and antipathies. The artist, consciously or unconsciously, approaches the threshold between the sensible and supersensible worlds and brings something back from the supersensible world into the world of the senses. The resulting creation is a specifically experienced reality lifted into a universal expression.

As Waldorf teachers we understand the importance of the arts and our own creativity in the work with our students. Can we also imagine applying a consciously artistic approach and a heightened sense of feeling to our work with our colleagues in our meetings?

Social Art

In the series of lectures *Art as Seen in the Light of Mystery Wisdom*,[8] Steiner connected each of the arts with the various members of the human being. The laws of the physical body, he said, are expressed in architecture, the etheric in sculpture, the astral in painting, and the ego in music. The still developing Spirit Self he connected to poetry and the Life Spirit to eurythmy. The highest art, according to Steiner, is social art.

The first three arts—architecture, sculpture, and painting (including drawing)—are the spatial arts. These are derived out of formative processes and past evolutionary cycles. They are connected to sculptural forces working out of the past and, in the context of education, help children come into their bodily constitution.

In contrast, the time arts—music, speech and poetry, and eurythmy—are connected to impulses coming out of the future. As Waldorf teachers we work out of our higher bodies and what Steiner called our musical forces in order to guide our students properly into their present life. Social art also belongs to this group of time arts, but is younger, less tangible, and even less developed than eurythmy. How can we study and practice this least tangible of arts?

My own experience is that working in any of the other arts can serve as a basic "instruction manual" for social art. Being grounded in an artistic practice makes it easier to apply the principles of creative activity to any aspect of life, including social situations.

As an early childhood teacher, when I had a particularly satisfying day in the kindergarten, I felt as if the children and I had spent the whole morning moving to an exquisite piece of music. When I was responsible for meetings, I began to plan agendas as if I were composing or painting and, during the meeting, I tried to pay attention to compositional elements like repetition, variation, contrast, harmony, balance, focus, surprise, and reprise.

In addition to the writings of Rudolf Steiner, we can also learn about social art in certain traditional texts where the renewing or healing spiritual element is represented symbolically: the "water of life" from the world of fairy tales, the Grail in the legend of Parsifal, the philosopher's stone of the alchemists, and conversation in Goethe's tale, "The Green Snake and the Beautiful Lily."

In North America we owe a great debt to Marjorie Spock, who brought Steiner's concern for community-building to us. She translated Steiner's *Awakening to Community* lectures into English and wrote two little pamphlets, entitled *Group Moral Artistry*, that are a continuing inspiration for many people. "Goethean Conversation" was the term she used to characterize the process by which a group could invite truth into their midst like a guest. She began with Goethe's framing of conversation as the art of arts and described Goethean conversation as a form of the reverse ritual and an appropriate means of practicing social artistry.

Artistic Meetings

Our artistic sensibilities and an artistic approach to our work in a meeting can enhance the possibility of lifting ourselves into the company of angels, if only briefly. Meetings can be artistic in a number of ways.

A meeting can become artistic when we consciously include an artistic activity in the agenda and allow what flows out of that activity to enhance the rest of our work together. It can also be artistic in the way we use imaginative pictures to enrich our conversations or moments of silence to invite creative inspirations. When the meeting itself is seen as an artistic process, the facilitator and the group will be more likely to strive for a palpable sense of aliveness and wholeness. Finally, if we take our work in the social art seriously, whatever we are able to achieve in the special situation of our meetings has the potential to strengthen our relationships overall and may even have a healing effect on other relationships in the community.

Conscious Conversation – An Invitation

We swim in a sea of spirit. Our matter-bound everyday consciousness, however, easily forgets the reality of spirit living in and everywhere around us. In this age of Michael especially, we have to wake up in those places where we are sleepily swept along with the materialistic tides of existence. It is not easy to push aside pressing everyday concerns again and again to make space for encounters with spirit in one another and with spirit beings on the other side of the threshold.

As Waldorf teachers, this is a task we have taken on not only for the sake of our students but also because the conversation with the spirit is the source of our own strength, inspiration, and creativity. In our meeting life and through an artistic practice of conscious conversation, we have an incredible opportunity to enter as a group into the realm of spirit-sensing.

Our own work as individuals—likewise the whole Waldorf movement—needs this renewing spiritual force as it continues to grow and proliferate in far-flung corners of the world.

Endnotes

1. Rudolf Steiner, *Awakening to Community* (Spring Valley, NY: Anthroposophic Press, 1974), p. 97.
2. Ibid., p. 157.
3. For a description of the Imagination, see *Foundations of Human Experience*, pp. 45–48.
4. Marjorie Spock, *Group Moral Artistry: Reflections on Community Building* (Spring Valley, NY: St. George Publications, 1983), p. 18.
5. Rudolf Steiner, *The Arts and Their Mission* (Spring Valley, NY: Anthroposophic Press, 1964), Lecture II.
6. Rudolf Steiner, *Art as Spiritual Activity*, Michael Howard, ed. Ch. 5: "The Two Sources of Art: Impressionism and Expressionism," Munich, Feb. 15, 1918 (Hudson, NY: Anthroposophic Press, 1998).
7. Ibid., Ch. 4: "Sense Organs and Aesthetic Experience," Dornach, Aug. 15, 1916.
8. Rudolf Steiner, *Art as Seen in the Light of Mystery Wisdom* (London: Rudolf Steiner Press, 1984).

The Three Castles and the Esoteric Life of the Teachers

Betty Staley

We live in a time when human beings are called upon to wake up and develop a new consciousness. Before the fifteenth century, prior to the birth of the consciousness soul, one could live out of one's natural development. There was still a feeling that beyond the physical world, spiritual beings were active and working with human beings. That has not been the case for the last five hundred years. More and more individuals have felt cut off and isolated from spiritual connections. In the nineteenth century Friedrich Nietzsche described it well with the expression "God is Dead." Spiritual beings have not disappeared, but they no longer take an active interest in the human being's physical development. Their work has been completed. Now, in the freedom we so value, we have the task of offering spiritual beings moral impulses that come out of our own efforts. Only then will they be interested. It is not destined that this will happen. It is up to us.

We have many choices in this age of freedom. We can choose to consciously awaken moral forces within ourselves or simply rely on traditions for moral guidance. We can be apathetic to moral forces stirring within, sleep through life unaware of choices available, or even work against moral forces by inviting forces of evil into our souls. We can see evidence of choices people make just by reading the daily newspaper.

Teachers have a special responsibility to understand and recognize the perilous situation of our time. Our task is to create and foster a relationship with our children that will help them find their true humanity, allowing them to make choices guided by an inner moral compass. In addition, we need to go beyond interest in students in our classroom to a concern for humanity at large, particularly in the context of the kinds of temptation that seek to weaken or even destroy the awakening ego of human souls.

Wolfram von Eschenbach, in his telling of *Parzival*, has laid before us great imaginations of this modern condition and the journey that the serious teacher can embark upon as a path of initiation. In the legend of Parzival, there are three castles—the Castle of King Arthur, the Castle of the Grail, and the Castle of Wonders. Parzival and Gawan, as twin seekers, represent the modern consciousness-soul human being journeying through the three castles on a path of initiation. When I refer to the three castles, I am using them as images of three different ways in which the teacher is challenged in his or her inner development.

Behind the Arthurian and the Parzival quests lie the deepest mysteries connected with the cosmic intelligence of Michael and soul transformation. Each mystery responds to the historical challenge of its time. In the path through the Castle of Wonders we have the possibility of transforming dark forces into light. There is no specific order in working with the three castles, since each relates to a particular aspect of what needs attention. The conscious integration of the three leads to healthy inner development. Through understanding what happens in each of these castles, the teacher can nurture his or her esoteric life in service of the Good.

The Castle of King Arthur –
Living in the sentient soul: finding ourselves in the social realm

There are many legends around King Arthur, and it can be confusing to figure out which depict the historical Arthur and which the legendary one. The name "Arthur" denoted an initiate who had reached the rank of leading one of the Mystery Schools that existed in pre-Christian times and continued until at least the ninth century. Richard Seddon describes the task of the Mystery School of Arthur as

> ...to carry into the Christian era the wisdom which the builders of the megaliths—during the previous age of Michael around 2500 BC—had acquired through their observations of the way the spiritual forces from sun, moon and planets varied in their passage through the zodiac. (p. 14)

Seddon points out that the name "Arthur" is Celtic, deriving from *Art-Hu. Art* means "to plough," and *Hu* is the Welsh name of the Sun God who descended to earth, known to us as the Christ. Thus the name "Arthur" is "the ploughman of the Sun God" relating the star wisdom with practical work on earth. As Virginia Sease puts it,

> Rudolf Steiner describes how Arthur and his knights experienced the sun in a quite specific way, and how they had experienced the Christ on the Sun before He left it in order to descend to earth. The Arthurian knights had taken up this experience of the Christ on the Sun in their own etheric bodies. ...They took the Christ into themselves. This created a foundation for their mission. They sent emissaries out across Europe in order to battle the wildness in the astral bodies of Europe's population, as well as to purify and civilize it. (p. 23)

René Querido adds to this picture:

The Celtic Stream, even as it embraced Christianity, had never forsaken the cosmos. Because of this, as the strength of the Grail impulse increased (about the fifth century AD), it became possible for a group of men to appear who represented the cosmic forces in such a way that they were able to fulfill a world destiny. These men were King Arthur and his Knights of the Round Table. They stood, with King Arthur as the Sun at their center and with each king so embodying the impulse of one of the zodiacal constellations that together they could act as a twelvefold whole. The Holy Grail was the ideal toward which their vision ever turned and which guided their deeds. As a Michael community they fought to ensure Michael's continued dominion over Cosmic Intelligence; they struggled against the severance of intelligence from Michael. They strove against the old demonic forces and on behalf of civilization. This community fought longer than any other that Michael should remain regent over Intelligence. This was the mission of the Arthurian Round Table. (p. 62)

As the knights of King Arthur took on the mission to purify astral bodies, we as teachers must take on that task for ourselves. It is in our work in the faculty that we are often challenged with the all-too-human qualities in our soul life: jealousy, envy, need for power, arrogance, judgment, gossip, and even a sense of martyrdom.

When we picture King Arthur and the Round Table, we imagine a castle occupied with knights and ladies dressed in elegant clothing, following the rules of chivalry. In order to become a knight of King Arthur, one had to perform brave deeds, defend ladies, and kill monsters. When Arthur traveled beyond the confines of his castle, he would lay down a silken cloth that represented the Round Table. Wherever Arthur went, he and his knights undertook noble deeds that brought law and order to the realm. Thus, within our classrooms we continue the connection to the Spiritual Being of the school that we cultivate in the faculty meeting and in our daily meditation.

This work is represented by the sphere of rights—the relationship of one to another in the social community. Those who belonged to it were a brotherhood. The Round Table was an image of the zodiac, with King Arthur as the sun, radiating order. He was the king, the head, out of which streamed forces of the sentient soul, of warmth and good fellowship, which illuminated the social life of the kingdom.

Faculty members act as the Court of King Arthur, gathering around the imagination of the Being of the school and the Being of Waldorf education, as Rudolf Steiner described it at the opening of the first Waldorf school:

My dear friends, It is our duty to be aware of the importance of our task. This we shall achieve if we realize that this school is to become the bearer of quite a special impulse. And so, first of all, we must direct our thoughts towards the consciousness that something special is to be borne into the world through this education. Such a realization will come about if we do not look upon this act of founding the school as an ordinary everyday event, but as a *festive act in the great ordering of the world*. In this sense I wish to take the first step by expressing the deepest gratitude in the name of the Great Spirit who is to lead mankind out of its present state of suffering and misery into a higher stage of development in education and training. …Let us look upon ourselves as human beings whom karma has brought to this place where something is to happen which shall surpass ordinary events—something which may make all participants here feel that they have witnessed a festive moment of world destiny. (*Towards the Deepening of Waldorf Education,* p. 53)

There are the special moments that occur in faculty meetings and meetings of the College of Teachers when we are attuned to one another, recognizing the tasks we have taken on, doing our inner work faithfully, and striving to serve the Being of the school. Then we can feel something new has entered human social life, something that is only a seed now but that carries the potential for future working. This must have been similar for Arthur who was trying to bring about a new world order based on justice and law rather than vengeance and power.

Each faculty is a gathering of teachers who have been brought together by karma. They are charged with working together as a brotherhood, a sisterhood, for the benefit of the children in the school. This is not easy. The social life is the warmth mantle that surrounds each school. We may feel it when we walk into a school building or onto the school grounds. We may sense through the care of the environment, the quality of the children's work, the way teachers greet each other, or the way teachers and parents relate, that something special lives here.

Today, social and antisocial forces work very strongly in this area. When we live in the sentient soul quality, we are experiencing our "I" through the sentient soul in which surge astral forces of sympathy and antipathy. There are times when we stand in our individuality and at the same time experience ourselves as a member of a group. Faculty members can experience themselves gathered around the table, inspired by the Spirit working into their hearts as into a spiritual vessel. But at other times they can experience small cliques of teachers, making decisions out of limited interest subgroups. For example, a school may be starting a high school. The class teachers say, "We can't spend so much money on the high school. There are so many more things we need in the elementary school. We have worked long and hard and deserve this." Or it might be the high school teachers who claim they work the hardest and therefore need to be paid more. Or the early childhood teachers claim they are the doorway to the school and need to have more time to strengthen their etheric bodies, and so forth. Rather than speaking as one of the circle, each person takes refuge in his or her group identity.

This also happens in relationships with parents. The teachers may hold themselves up as the experts and say, "We teachers know about this because we know anthroposophy, but you parents don't understand it," or "The College of Teachers has made this decision, but we cannot share the process with you because everything we talk about is sacred and secret."

The esoteric life of the teacher in relation to King Arthur's castle is to learn to be a true social being, bringing nobility and orderliness to the school community.

After Arthur was crowned king, he set about righting the wrongs that had been done in England since the death of Uther Pendragon. He forced those who had wrongfully taken the land of others to return it to the rightful owners. He set free many prisoners who were unjustly held. He demanded that all should obey the laws of the realm. (Sterne, p. 19)

How would Arthur battle for his kingdom? The initiate Merlin guided him to a shining blue lake.

In the middle of the lake, Arthur saw an arm clothed in white samite, mysterious and wonderful. High above the blue water, the raised arm held a sword encased in a rich scabbard embellished all in gold. Arthur asked the Lady of the Lake for the sword, for he had none of his own. "Sir Arthur, King of England, the sword Excalibur is mine. If you will give me a gift when I ask it, you shall have the sword." Arthur agreed and rowed out to the center of the lake and reached for the sword Excalibur. At his touch the hand let go the hilt, and hand and arm sank slowly under the water. (Sterne, pp. 26–27)

Arthur's sword came from the supersensible world in order to aid in his mission on earth. Arthur was guided from infancy by Merlin, his protector and guide, whose task was to serve the good. In a similar way did Rudolf Steiner speak to the teachers of the Waldorf school when he said: "In the evenings before your meditation, ask the Angels, Archangels and Archai that they may help you in your work on the following day." (Recollections of Caroline von Heydebrand and Walter Johannes Stein, in *Towards the Deepening of Waldorf Education*, p. 62)

Teachers in Waldorf schools often hold the ideal of Waldorf education in the highest place, even as a utopia. However, the difference between the ideal and the real can be very frustrating. To keep striving for the ideal can become a daily mantra. Yet one cannot have blinders on to what is happening between people in the confusions of everyday life. The ideal can create distance between colleagues, one of whom may judge the other as being "more Waldorf." As we follow the Arthurian legends, we find that Camelot, the city Merlin had built using all the arts his magic could command, was also subject to human failings. Despite the ideals Arthur had so valiantly required of his Round Table and of those in his castle, the transgressions of Guinevere and Lancelot, the hatred of Modred, and the quick retreat from forgiveness to vengeance made Camelot disappear from the earthly realm and continue only as an intention, as a hope for the future.

To be realistic, we can't live in paradise on the physical plane. To think that one can is an illusion. And yet our times demand that we strive to be social, recognizing that we have both social and anti-social forces working in our souls. But despite the challenges, we must keep trying to develop ourselves as social beings.

What does it mean to be a social being when we are constantly aware of anti-social forces in our own thinking, as well as in the thoughts of others around us?

When we listen to another person, we are often not really listening, but instead we are thinking about our own response. We want to let the other person know what is on our mind. In order to hold on to our own thought, we resist what the other person is saying. We don't want our own thoughts to be overshadowed by the other person's words. We resist the tendency of our thinking to be put to sleep by the other person. A small battle rages between speaker and listener. But even if our thinking is put to sleep, our feeling and willing are not. In the contrast between our own thoughts and the speaker's, we wake up to ourselves. If we did not, we would go along with whatever the speaker said and we would lose self-awareness. For the modern person, this would be intolerable. This dynamic between two people is mostly unconscious, but at times we become aware of how anti-social we really are, and we can hardly help it. Our own sense of self-love encourages us to make our own point known, whether by nodding or shaking our head in agreement or disagreement, or by stating our position without letting the other person finish a thought.

While half of our soul life is anti-social, the other half is social. Rudolf Steiner tells us that, when we are asleep at night, we are meeting each other and are united socially. There are no boundaries between us. However, the moment we wake up, we begin to develop our conceptual life, and anti-social impulses come streaming in. Sitting in a meeting, we feel that we already know what our colleagues are going to say, so we don't really need to listen. We build a wall around ourselves, knowing with certainty that we are right and the speaker is wrong. Most of us don't think we walk around harboring pre-judgments or prejudices, but they are working unconsciously.

What shall we do to bring a social impulse to this situation? We have to consciously master these anti-social forces, recognizing that people are not fixed but are always developing. We have to respect freedom of thought and not impose our thoughts on someone else. We have to allow people to question us without becoming our enemies.

The faculty develops the structure of the castle, the Round Table, which establishes the working relationships between the different members. The structure that is established allows for processes to take place. The structure may be hierarchical or horizontal. It may be constituted of committees with clear mandates given to each committee, or it may be administratively centralized. However it is organized, there should be clear processes that are agreed upon so that the group knows how to deal with issues as they come up. Having clear processes helps keep antipathy from getting out of hand. The anti-social forces wake us up; they are part of the modern condition in which we treasure our independence, standing up for what we want. However, we need to look beyond our own desires to the life of the community and help create processes to bring balance and order. For example, what structure exists so that parents can voice a grievance without thinking the teacher will take it out on their child? What processes are there to evaluate an assembly without a teacher feeling attacked or at least unappreciated? What structure is in place for mandates? What forms of appreciation recognize people's efforts? How can we learn to be critical without attacking? How do we work with principles of conflict resolution?

In our feeling life we tend to distort the picture we have of another person, and negative feelings rise up. We are tossed back and forth between sympathy and antipathy. We can love one another for a brief time, but after that, something comes up, maybe from a past meeting, and we become critical and judgmental. Sometimes we aren't even conscious that this is happening. How can we bring healthy social forces to bear?

We must learn to know the other person more deeply so we can broaden the image we have been holding of him or her. Since most of our judgments are based on sympathy and antipathy, we have to go beyond them to a new understanding. Out of interest we must get to know the other faculty member better; what is the person interested in, what was his childhood like, what does she feel passionate about? How can we help a new teacher feel a sense of belonging with the group? Is there a good balance in the rights sphere between equality for all and times when an individual case needs to be considered differently?

In our will life we are also influenced by sympathies and antipathies. Our idealism can justify a feeling of self-righteousness. When two colleagues hold to competing ideals which lead to different decisions, it is important to recognize that each one wants what is best for the children and society. Trying to find a third way may lift the issue out of the personal. Other colleagues can be helpful in resolving such a social problem.

We love a particular person because he or she does what we would do, or we dislike the person who does things differently. Most of the time when we think we're expressing love for another person, we are actually engaged in the illusion of love; it is really self-love. We feel proud that we sacrificed something of ourselves for the other person, but if we are really honest, we find we liked the feeling in ourselves of giving, enjoyed our own sense of generosity. It is a case of masked egoism, and we need to use self-discipline and self-reflection to overcome the feeling of being self-satisfied.

The challenge of operating in King Arthur's castle is to live horizontally, with the image of the King as the Being of the school. Of course, there may be hierarchical roles, but those are agreed to by the group. The true hierarchy is a spiritual one. The biggest challenge in this castle is the maturing of our social life in the consideration of the good of the whole.

Anything that prevents the human Ego from working out of the social forces holds us back. We need to put the interests of the other before those of self-interest as a new way of working. In King Arthur's time, the knights rode out into the forests to fight monsters. In our time we have to wake up to the monsters within and, in the way we work, make room for something higher to enter.

The Grail Castle –
Living in the heart-mind soul

The Grail Castle is different from the castle of King Arthur. In order to enter it, one has to cross a bridge over a moat, leaving everyday life behind and passing into the spiritual world. Parzival stumbled into it when he was seeking his mother, not knowing she had died. Parzival did not understand anything about the Grail Castle. He was amazed by it, but he did not ask any questions.

Later, the hermit Trevrizent explained to Parzival the rules of the Grail Castle and its connection with the Grail King, Anfortas. When the former Grail King, Frimurtel (Trevrizent's father) lost his life, his eldest son, Anfortas, was chosen to succeed him as king and Lord of the Grail and the Grail's company. As Anfortas came into his manhood, he left the Castle in search of excitement and adventure. The rule was that if any Lord of the Grail craved a love other than the one whose name came up on the Grail writing, he would suffer distress and grievous misery.

Anfortas went against his duty and was filled with passion for a particular woman. He bravely fought for her and won great fame and, in doing that, became prideful. This also violated the code of behavior, which required moderation in all things. His desires led him further and further in search of adventure to prove his manhood to the woman, and eventually he was wounded in the testicles with a poisoned spear by a heathen who sought the Grail for its power. Anfortas was still the King of the Grail, but he was wounded and could not carry out his responsibilities.

Of course, none of this was known to Parzival. However, he saw that the king was suffering, he saw a strange procession with squires carrying a bleeding lance, and he heard members of the castle moaning in deep anguish. He remembered only that Gurnemanz had told him not to talk so much, and so he did not ask any questions.

As Parzival continued on his journey, he slowly began to wake up. After meeting Sigune and recognizing that he had failed in not asking the question, "he felt a deep remorse ... that he had been so slow to question as he sat by the side of the sorrowful host. His self-reproaches and the heat of the day brought the sweat pouring from him." (Book V)

When we recognize that we have missed an opportunity with a student, a colleague, or a parent, we may feel overwhelmed with guilt. Why was I asleep? Will there be another opportunity? How can I heal this situation? As with Parzival, we can also be asleep to another person's pain and suffering. A child in our class may have gone through a difficult experience, but we did not notice it. Perhaps his favorite pet died or perhaps her grandmother became very ill. When we find out later, we may realize we had not been a careful observer and had missed an important opportunity to support the child.

Parzival tries to make up for his thoughtless behavior with Jeschute when he forces Orilus to reconcile with his wife. "Then Parzival did as a man who is true must do. He took the holy casket and swore an oath upon it of his own free will. And he framed the oath thus, 'Upon my honor as a knight—whether I have the honor myself or not, whoever sees me bear my shield will know me a member of knighthood's order—the power of this name, so the code of chivalry teaches us, has often won great fame and its name is still exalted today. May I stand disgraced forever before the world and all my honor be lost, and as pledge for these words let my happiness, with my deeds, be offered here before the Hand Supreme that, I believe, God bears. May I suffer shame and scorn forever by His power, in body and in soul, if this lady did do anything amiss when I snatched her brooch from her and took her golden ring as well. I was a fool then, not a man, and not yet grown to wisdom.' " (Book V)

When we look back upon our day during a "Review of the Day" exercise, we can re-experience our actions. At times we may feel the kind of shame that Parzival felt, and out of that embarrassment we may vow to ourselves to heal whatever pains we have caused. I well remember Cecil Harwood, one of the teachers in my Waldorf training, speaking about the mistakes we would make as young teachers. He told us that, at the beginning of our teaching career, the angels of the children would forgive our mistakes as long as we had enthusiasm. As we gained experience, we would become more personally responsible for our actions and might suffer because of our lost opportunities and feel guilt.

In Book VI three very important events happen that serve as guidance for the teacher in relation to spiritual practice. At the very moment when Parzival is reaching his goal, to become a member of the Round Table, Kundry publicly accuses him of the sinful deed of not asking the question of the wounded king in the Grail Castle. "The fame and power of the Round Table are lamed now that Sir Parzival has joined its company, though he also bears, as he sits over there, the outward signs of a knight. ...A curse on the beauty of your face and on your manly limbs. ...May your mouth become empty, I mean of the tongue within it, as your heart is empty of real feeling! You adder's fang!" Parzival, shamed, leaves the Round Table to seek the Grail and make amends.

Another knight, Gawan, is wrongfully accused of killing a man and must face battle against a powerful enemy. The chivalric code requires that he respond to such a challenge even though he is innocent. He, too, must leave the Round Table.

Despite the pain that the knights experience in this scene, they learn about the existence of Parzival's half-brother, and they learn about the Castle of Wonders where four hundred maidens and four queens are held captive. In addition to the pain, the new relationship between Parzival and Gawan becomes one of joy and fulfillment that will carry them through the next stages of their journey.

In Book IX Parzival crosses a threshold into maturity. He meets Trevrizent and realizes he needs help. "Parzival the warrior dismounted at once, and standing with great modesty before him, he told of the people who had shown him the way and how they had praised the hermit's counsels. Then he said, 'Sir, now give me counsel. I am a man who has sinned.' "

After Parzival learns of his lineage, of the deaths he has caused, and of his relationship with Trevrizent, he confesses and begs forgiveness. Trevrizent's reply is one that should be helpful to us when we realize our mistakes: "And you must not grieve too much. You should in right measure grieve and abstain from grief." As we take responsibility for our imperfections, we also need to forgive ourselves and go forward rather than live too strongly in self-recrimination.

The Grail Castle represents the scene of the Intellectual or Heart-Mind Soul. The seeker who enters the Grail Castle is challenged to spiritualize the thinking forces. Over time man's thinking has become more and more dead, rigid, and cold, guided by old traditions and custom. With a one-sided development of intelligence, human thinking has given way to pride, haughtiness, and cruelty. The materialistic influence on thinking has led people to intellectualism. While objectivity and clear thinking are a necessary part of the Heart-Mind Soul, the challenge of the Grail Castle is to enter on the path of developing capacities of perception. That is our challenge as teachers.

When we enter the realm of the Grail Castle in our Heart-Mind Soul, we find we are interconnected with other people in our lives. We are given the opportunities in daily practice to grow spiritually as we transform our thinking, strengthening our connections with the spiritual world and shaping our daily lives in alignment with our higher self. As we work more and more out of individual freedom rather than rules of conduct, we expand our soul capacities so that the work of the Heart-Mind Soul is transformed into Consciousness Soul activity.

The events connected with all aspects of the Grail Castle have consequence for the esoteric life of the teacher. It is both a lonely path and a path we take with others. Our inner, meditative life is one that we develop between the hierarchies and ourselves. In our meditation we relate to the spiritual hierarchies every night.

- How I carried out my thought life during the day determines the way I enter the presence of the Angels.
- How I used my speech during the day determines whether I come worthily to the Archangels.
- How I used my movement during the day determines whether I come worthily near to the Archai.

In our daily behavior we must seek equanimity rather than excess. Moderation and humility help us as we stand in awe before the child, asking: "Who are you? What is your destiny? How can I serve you?" Steiner's Six Basic Exercises or the Eightfold Path of Buddha can help us in this development.

Each teacher is responsible for acting out of the wisdom of transformed thinking and out of a balanced feeling life in interaction with a group of colleagues, with parents, and with children. We embody this meaning when the teachers are asked to:

Imbue yourself with the power of imagination,
Have courage for the truth,
Sharpen your feeling for responsibility of Soul.
            (cf. Steiner, *Study of Man*, p. 190)

In our esoteric practice we must strive for the truth. There will be times when we feel wrongly judged by a colleague or parent. We have to wrestle with the wish to prove ourselves right, to strike back, to find some certainty in the midst of unknowingness. To strive for the truth without needing to demean or destroy the other is the challenge here. Opening ourselves to the gifts of others helps us to appreciate those we may have previously misunderstood.

In our work with the children, it is important to recognize that the soul of a growing child has come down to earth from a previous incarnation. The child is not an accident, nor a mere product of genes. Our observation of the child and the child study we carry out in our faculty meetings lay the basis for our insights of how to work with each child. We can honor the gifts and challenges that come from the past. Through spiritualizing our thinking about the child, we build a picture of the child and his or her needs. Then we can understand that our task is to help clear away obstacles so that the child may meet his or her own destiny.

As we work with children, parents, and colleagues, our thoughts must go beyond our family, racial, and national roots. The path to the Grail is a spiritualized Christianity (in the broadest sense of the word) that welcomes all religions and all people. One truth has many aspects.

As Parzival is nearing the Grail Castle at the end of his journey, he meets Feirefis, his half-brother. Parzival is told he must choose a companion to accompany him. Although Feirefis is born of a Muslim mother and Christian father, and is himself a pagan owing loyalty to many gods and goddesses, he is the one who is chosen. Von Eschenbach is pointing to a future when a particular religion will no longer be the defining authority for transformation.

We are not only traversing our individual path, but we are deeply connected with our colleagues, the staff, the children, and their families. It is not a matter of our reaching a higher stage of development for its own sake. Once we have reached a certain stage on the inner path, we have to remember to take our brothers and sisters with us. There is no salvation for as long as even a single fellow human being remains excluded.

At different times in the legend, we see the importance of balance between the masculine and feminine in developing our higher self. Parzival could not have awakened to his task without the help of Sigune and Kundry. Gawan needed the wisdom of the frozen queen (his grandmother), the challenge of the feisty Orgilus, and the tenderness of the ferryman's daughter Bene to become a complete person. We do not work in our own king- (or queen-)doms. Every teacher, every staff member helps us on our way.

Those who approach the Grail must ask questions. This is an attitude of soul as we work together in a school. We may not have the answers, but we need to learn to ask the right questions. Sometimes the questions are uninvited, they stir up tension, but they serve the purpose of clearing a path to Truth. The path for the teacher who enters the Grail Castle is a lonely, individual path to transform ordinary thinking into spiritual communion. Then the transformed thinking can become a resource for the transformation of the school.

In Volume 8 of *Karmic Relationships*, Rudolf Steiner writes:

There ... stands King Arthur's castle where men still turn to the Cosmic Intelligence and where they strive to instill the Intelligence belonging to the universe into civilization on earth. And [there] stands that other castle, the Grail castle, where the Intelligence is no longer drawn from the heavens but where it is realized that what is wisdom before men is foolishness before God and what is wisdom before God is foolishness before men. (p. 39)

The intelligence of the Grail Castle is found on earth, no longer flowing from the heavens. It is here in our everyday earthly activity that we do our spiritual work. It is the inner path of meditation in which we deepen our connection to the world outside and the world within. Parzival had to learn these lessons also in order to transform his thinking and be genuinely ready to stand before the Grail King and ask the question.

The Castle of Wonders –
Entering into the consciousness soul

The Castle of Wonders with its surrounding region signifies the deepest mysteries of the laws of karma and reincarnation. Each of us has a Castle of Wonders: the dark places in our soul where shadows lurk and ugliness confronts us. We can also call it a Castle of Wounds, since we each carry the hurts from childhood and youth (as well as from past life experience) into our adult life. Often we choose not to enter this castle because it is so painful, and yet we must if we are to follow the path of the consciousness soul—the path where Gawan enters into initiation. To be able to enter the Castle of King Arthur and transform our social life, and to enter the Castle of the Grail and transform our thinking life, we must take the steps and face our will and our feelings in the Castle of Wonders. However, in addition to painful experiences bound up with the Castle of Wonders, there are also the possibilities of healing and joy. Many of the steps we take in this region are unconscious. We meet people to whom we owe karmic debts as well as those who need to offer us healing. This is the region where the ordering of karma can be set in motion.

In the Parzival legend, Gawan enters a new realm and is quickly filled with passion for a woman who scorns him. He sees beyond her outer appearance and he shows restraint and patience. After he has shown compassion to an injured knight and risked his life for her, the woman's mask is dropped, and a real love awakens in her. As Gawan continues moving through this land of wonders, he notices that everything is topsy-turvy and it is hard to figure out what is what. This is often true with karma.

As he is on his way to the Grail (a task given to him as penance), he reaches the ferryman's house and has to cross over a river to enter into the kingdom of the Castle of Wonders. Gawan has now entered into his soul world where he will meet unbalanced aspects of himself and evil forces lurking to envelop him. This is his path of initiation. In contrast to Parzival who didn't ask the question, Gawan asks why the four hundred maidens were locked in the castle, but he is told not to ask. When he persists in trying to find out why, the ferryman lends him a shield and tells him to arm himself.

As teachers, when we decide to enter into our own soul world, we need certain protection so that we can keep our center in the midst of travail. To serve life means we will be severely tested.

The ferryman tells Gawan to leave his horse outside and meet the trader, who tells him that if he succeeds he will receive all the wealth of the kingdom. When we enter the dark parts of our soul where imbalance and evil forces live, we have to go alone. Inside the castle are all the enemies of the Grail (of spiritualized thinking). When we overcome these forces, we receive the wealth of Oneness, of Completeness of body, soul, and spirit. The castle is fortified on all sides. How hard it is for us to take up the journey of initiation. Strong walls protect our vulnerability and flaws. Do we have the courage to carry on?

As Gawan enters the castle, he sees the huge wonder bed shifting back and forth, and it is hard for him to jump onto it and claim it. He leaps into the middle of it, and it thunderously bangs back and forth against the walls. When the bed comes to a stop, Gawan is shaken and doesn't know what is coming next. The Castle of Wonders concerns the Word, the Truth. The banging of the bed might be like our tongue moving. There is an Arabic saying, "While the word is yet unspoken, you are master of it; when once it is spoken, it is master of you."

When we begin the path of initiation, it is difficult to get a handle on the tasks. One may try this or that, but it is too hard to focus, to carry out our intention in practice. We may decide it isn't worth the effort to master our will, it's too hard, and we return to past ways of relating. Then our work becomes hollow, for we are no longer allowing an opening for the spirit to shine, the angel of the child to guide us, the Being of the school to illumine us.

Back in the Castle of Wonders, Gawan is pelted with stones from five hundred slingshots, so much so that his shield is dented. Five hundred arrows are aimed at him as well.

Often when we enter the soul world, we find people attack us, misunderstand us, and try to manipulate us. We have to master our will and not react unthinkingly. We say to ourselves, "Patience, heart, patience." There are many ways we keep on the armor so we won't experience the stones and arrows— self-medicating through drugs or alcohol, losing ourselves in television, computer programs or social media, promiscuity, numbing our feeling life, or even leaving the school because we don't have the courage to face ourselves.

One of the most common means by which we get in our own way is through denial. Perhaps through our mentor or an evaluator, observations are made of our work, along with suggestions. It is difficult and painful to hear criticism. But how do we handle it? Do we welcome it as a way to continue growing? Do we deny it? Do we blame a few parents who have launched complaints against us? Do we say we were never told about these problems before? Do we go on attack, rallying half of the class parents to our side, accusing the school of unfairness? Legitimate questions are put to the school: Are processes in place to help a teacher meet difficult situations? What kind of support is there? What is objective evaluation?

Often one finds that a teacher who has difficulty in one school may have had the same problem elsewhere. The problem may take time to surface, but it will come out. It is another call for the teacher to take the problem seriously and do the soul work involved.

Gawan is beaten up by a thug, and then a huge lion attacks him. Gawan manages to cut off its leg, but he is wounded too and is losing blood. He manages to kill the lion before falling unconscious. He has almost lost the battle. It isn't a complete win because he is badly injured.

In addition to the wounds from our childhood and youth, we bear the wounds of our adult experiences. Colleagueship issues can wound, friendships can become betrayals, and lovers can become enemies. Do we retaliate or do we master our will and our words? Are we going to carry our wounds to our grave or begin to heal them?

The mystery of the relationship between the Castle of Wonders and the Grail Castle is expressed when Arnive, the elderly queen, who is caring for Gawan's wounds says, "I will quickly bring you relief. Kundry *la sorciere* is kind enough to come and see me frequently, and whatever may be done with medicines she imparts to me. Ever since Anfortas has been in such wretched pain so that he was in need of help, this salve has aided in keeping him from death; it came from Munsalvaesche [the Grail castle]."

By conquering the Castle of Wonders, Gawan becomes the master of the region, the queens and ladies are freed from their spell, and he goes out and battles knights and proves his love for Orgeluse. When he stands up to her taunting, Gawan reclaims himself. Orgeluse in turn is freed from her anger and sarcasm. She tells him how her lover Cidegast was slain by King

Gramoflanz, from whom Gawan has just taken the wreath, and then continues to tell him the secret behind Anfortas' wounding, of Clinschor's evil, and of the bravery of the Red Knight who refused her love. Having healed the karmic knot, Gawan and Orgeluse return to the castle and are welcomed by the enchanted ladies.

Gawan has become master of himself as well as master of the Castle of Wonders. Now he has the presence of mind to ask Arnive, the elder, about the origins of Clinschor's magical powers. Arnive tells him the secrets behind Clinschor's evil actions and how she and the other maidens had fallen under his power. But now that Gawan is master over Clinschor's land, everything can return to its previous harmony.

The maidens and the elder queens are now freed. Before, the feminine forces had been held hostage, frozen in time. When they are released, they can care for Gawan and bring him back to health. All who were frozen are freed to meet once again and deepen their relationships. We can ask ourselves: What is frozen in our soul life? What needs to be freed?

Without the freeing of the feminine, Gawan cannot allow his heart to rule. But he does heal his heart so that he will be able to give to others and rule with love and compassion. He is now the master of the Castle of Wonders, and in so becoming, all the women are freed. What a picture for us as we work on the negative forces in our soul life—bringing courage and heart-warmth to our inner struggle, thus freeing the forces of love for others!

The Castle of Wonders is entangled in mystery, miscommunication, and danger. This is expressed in the difficulty Gawan faces in his battle with Gramoflanz. His sister Itonje is in love with Gramoflanz, even though they have never met. However, Gawan is set to battle Gramoflanz. If he succeeds, his sister will be devastated. If Gramoflanz wins,

Itonje will be devastated at the loss of her brother. Orgeluse wants Gramoflanz defeated because of the way he wounded her in the past. Gawan wants to defeat Gramoflanz to prove his love for Orgeluse. There seems to be no way out. To make matters worse, Gawan invites Arthur to bring the whole Round Table to observe the battle and celebrate his winning and his wedding. This situation is fraught with tragedy.

However, the elders step in with their wisdom. King Brandelidelin (Gramoflanz' uncle) sits by Ginover (Guinevere) the Queen and speaks with her. Arthur then leads Brandelidelin away to the tent, shares a drink, and lays out the situation. King Brandelidelin understands. "Sir, it is our sisters' children who will face each other in hatred. We must prevent the battle. There can be only one outcome, that they love each other with true affection. Your niece Itonje should first bid my nephew give up the battle for her sake, if he desires her love. Thus the battle, with all its strife, will be avoided completely. And do you also help my nephew to win the favor of the duchess."

"That I will do," says Arthur. "Gawan, my sister's son, has enough power over her that she, finely bred as she is, will leave to the two of us, to him and to me, the settlement of the issue. And you then make peace on your side." (Book XIV) Through this action of the elders, reconciliation takes place.

Self-mastery of the Word cautions us to avoid gossip, complaint, criticism, cynicism, backbiting, and even feigned politeness when life or the world seems painful, unpleasing, or difficult. Mastery of the Word calls for us to be authentic. Clinschor, the Black magician, created the Castle of Wonders out of a desire for revenge, out of jealousy, anger, and hatred. Gawan has to transform these feelings and become the master of the Will and thus free Clinschor as well as himself and the rest of the kingdom. Such feelings live in our souls, too. If we transform them, the shadows in our soul, the Clinschor in us gives up his power and the negative feelings can become kindness, courtesy, healing, courage, commitment, and love. We can point to the journey through the Castle of Wonders as a therapeutic path.

Conclusion

There is a question that is left hanging in the Parzival legend. Could Parzival have healed Anfortas if Gawan had not mastered the Castle of Wonders?

Parzival is traveling the lonely journey to find the Grail castle again and to ask the question of Anfortas, the wounded Grail King. It is not a matter of knowing what words to ask. Parzival has had to undergo soul transformation so that when he asks the question, it comes out of a deep longing born of soul sorrow. He has to be authentic. However, behind the scenes, Gawan heals the karmic entanglement of Anfortas and Clinschor. I believe this is also necessary in order for Parzival to fulfill his destiny. Parzival represents the conscious search for wholeness and healing. Gawan represents the healing of what is broken so that the next step in initiation can take place. Reconciliation, love, and healing are essential if we are to go forward and carry out our destiny.

As Waldorf teachers we are also on the path of the three castles. We live in the Arthurian castle when we create Waldorf schools that are harmonious and orderly. We live in the Grail castle when we work on our meditative life. We live in the transformed Castle of Wonders when we heal karmic problems that keep us from being free to go forward in the future.

The path of the three castles is an esoteric path for teachers to transform their soul forces. In each castle we meet ourselves on a different level—on the social, in our thinking, and in our soul challenges. The three paths become one path, entwining thinking, feeling, and will as they interact and create a vessel for the "I." In the crowning moments when the three join as one, we become the new kings of ourselves, and we are able to represent the spiritual task of Waldorf education.

Note: The terms Sun-Being, Great Spirit, and Time Spirit are used at times to refer to the Christ in the spiritual world, and not specifically to Christianity as a religion.

References

Querido, René. *The Mystery of the Holy Grail.* Fair Oaks, CA: Rudolf Steiner College Publications, 1991.

Sease, Virginia and Manfred Schmidt-Brabant. *Thinkers, Saints, Heretics: Spiritual Paths of the Middle Ages.* Forest Row, Sussex: Temple Lodge, 2007.

Seddon, Richard. "The Matter of Britain: Arthur, the Grail and Parzival," in *The Golden Blade,* No. 47. Edinburgh: Floris Books, 1994.

Towards the Deepening of Waldorf Education, excerpts from the work of Rudolf Steiner, *Essays and Documents,* Third Edition. Dornach, Switzerland: Pedagogical Section of the School of Spiritual Science, Goetheanum, 2006.

Steiner, Rudolf. *Karmic Relationships,* Volume 8. London: Rudolf Steiner Press, 1975.

Steiner, Rudolf. *The Mysteries of the East and of Christianity.* London: Rudolf Steiner Press, 1972.

Sterne, Emma Gelders and Barbara Lindsay. *Retelling of King Arthur and the Knights of the Round Table.* New York: Golden Press, 1962.

Von Eschenbach, Wolfram, *Parzival.* New York: Random House, 1961.

"Spirit Is Never without Matter; Matter Never without Spirit"[1]

A Narrative Examination of a College of Teachers

Liz Beaven

———————————

What makes a school a Waldorf school? This apparently straightforward question evokes a range of responses that embraces both physical aspects of our schools and the less tangible forces that frame and shape our work. A College of Teachers is often identified as one core characteristic that makes a school "Waldorf." Standing at the center of many of our schools, the College forms an essential part of the organizational structure, assuming a wide range of practical and less visible responsibilities and tasks. A College of Teachers is thereby continuously confronted with the challenge of balancing the spiritual and practical life of the school, a challenge that individual schools have met in a variety of ways. An examination of the function and role of a College can shed considerable light on the history and development of a school, its values, and the method by which it meets the challenges of mission, time, and place.

What follows is an attempt to focus attention in some depth on the College of Teachers of a particular school. This study grew out of discussions with colleagues from a number of schools as we all confronted organizational and governance challenges, and my resulting belief that it could be instructive to examine the inception and evolution of one College. Despite the influences of geography, biography, and personality on each school and the necessity for each one to develop its own unique form of organization and governance, Waldorf schools, like other institutions, display lawfulness and commonalities in their development. They pass through predictable phases as they move from fledgling impulse to mature, established school. Therefore, although there is no standard model or template for the creation or development of a school's governance and College, it is likely that most will encounter shared issues and challenges and therefore the lessons of one may help clarify process for another. It is hoped that readers of this study will find both helpful insights and cautionary tales in threads that are instantly recognizable to them, as well as aspects that are truly unique to the biography and destiny of one particular school. In this way, both commonalities and differences will allow schools to reflect on their own evolution and form.

The following description is centered on the College of Teachers at the Sacramento Waldorf School. The school has several features that make it a good candidate for such a study. It is a mature, established K–12 school—in its fifty-third year— and, aside from one night, has had a College of Teachers for forty-two of those years. The school re-founded its College over ten years ago as part of substantial changes in governance arising from a crisis brought on by growth and changing needs. The re-founding resulted in a much greater separation of the practical and spiritual aspects of College work than had previously been the case. The school has continued to refine and explore this separation as further questions have arisen, additional lessons have been learned, and needs have changed.

The story of this College of Teachers commences with a brief history of the school and the founding and development of its College. It describes the conditions and process that led to the re-founding, experiences since re-founding, a summary of lessons learned and questions to be answered, and a look to the future. Content was drawn from unpublished memoirs, many years of College minutes, governance documents and reports, conversations with current and former College members, and my own involvement with the school for almost twenty-one years. Although I made every attempt to check statements and validate the pictures as they emerged, the resulting description is inevitably subjective and incomplete, as it is viewed and reported through the lens of its author. As author, I have a personal attachment to this story: I have been a member of the school's College of Teachers since the late 1990s and was very actively involved in the process of re-founding. I have served as the school's administrator since 2001. My perspective of the College's story changed when I joined it in the late 1990s, and this change is captured in the article through a change of voice, from third person observer and reporter to first person participant.

Beginnings: Foundations and Growth

The Sacramento Waldorf School was founded in 1959, opening on October 7 of that year as a two-child kindergarten. Early records and individual recollections suggest that there was not a great deal of anthroposophical knowledge among the founding parents and board members; rather, with the exception of one anthroposophist, the founding impulse and primary focus was to establish a viable alternative education for their children. Even for many of the early faculty members, anthroposophy appeared to be a new and rather unfamiliar path (as reported in unpublished memoirs and conversations).

The school initially grew quite rapidly, expanding "from two to forty-two in less than a year."[2] Hermann von Baravalle, a Waldorf teacher from Germany who was involved in the early years of several schools in the U.S., guided the school's pedagogy and teacher training during its founding and early years but, although its guiding principles were imparted, the word *anthroposophy* was seldom mentioned. Within a short period of time, despite an early, encouraging pattern of growth, dissension emerged as to the orientation and purpose of the school, and there were signs of division and distress. The fledgling school lost many students as a result of this tension and looked to be in danger of collapse. The Board, seeking to save the school, turned for advice to Stewart Easton, another leading figure in the early days of Waldorf education. (Easton had previously visited the school and was familiar with it.)

As a result of his interest, the school recruited and invited a group of five young teachers, each of whom had participated in various anthroposophical teacher training programs and were experienced Waldorf pedagogues, to move from the East Coast to Sacramento and take up work at the school. They in turn were seeking a setting in which they could deepen their anthroposophical studies and work more fully and directly from Steiner's indications. They agreed to the move on condition that the faculty would be granted full control over all pedagogical matters and that the Board would pay off a debt incurred by the installation of some prefabricated buildings. Both demands were agreed upon and these young teachers, known in the school's history as the "Kimberton Five," arrived in 1965, essentially to re-found the school. Several teachers who had left returned soon after this point and enrollment began to build once again. The "Kimberton Five" would be extremely influential in the direction and growth of the school and in determining its spiritual and philosophical orientation.

Francis Edmunds, the founder of Emerson College in England, visited the young school each year as part of a grand sweep of the seven mainland American Waldorf schools in existence at that time. Edmunds had taught two of the young teachers and, along with Easton, was a trusted mentor and advisor. During one of his annual visits, he recommended the formation of a College of Teachers to further develop foundational anthroposophical work and thereby add vitality and depth to the school. Records suggest that this was still an unusual step for the young North American schools at that time, but in 1969 under his guidance and in his presence, the first College of Teachers was formed. Membership of this new group was open to any full-time member of the faculty who felt called to take up a new level of spiritual work as part of a circle of colleagues. The "Kimberton Five" and several others teachers stepped forward and began the tradition of College work on behalf of the school.[3]

The College of Teachers immediately became a core element of the school. From its inception, it was an integral part of the school's leadership, linked to the Board of Trustees through representative membership.[4] Bylaws from that time indicate that the Chairman of the faculty (soon redefined as the Chairman of the College of Teachers) and two faculty members nominated by the new College would serve as Trustees—comprising almost one-third of the Board's membership. During those early years the Board was busy supporting the physical needs of the growing school and was much occupied with site questions, building campaigns, and the management of inadequate budgets. True to the commitment made to the "Kimberton Five," the College maintained oversight of all pedagogical matters and engaged in developing program and curriculum, eventually pursuing the path to the foundation of a high school fifteen years after the school had opened. A search for a permanent home, the establishment of a high school, the constant need for more space, efforts to balance budgets and build enrollment—familiar terrain for those of us who have been involved in the development of Waldorf schools—fueled a great deal of common striving that united Board and College into the 1980s and inspired members to actively address critical questions and work side by side.

During these years of intense, often physical work and growth, the College continued to steer the pedagogical life of the school and to manage many of its practical business aspects. In those early years, support staff was limited; formal administrative support beyond basic clerical help was added in the early 1980s, and a more comprehensive administrative staff grew from that time forward, offering some relief to both College and Board.

Despite this step, the scope of the College's work remained considerable. Several individuals who were members from the 1980s into the early 1990s highlighted similar themes in their recollections. Members experienced the weight of their huge responsibility for the school. College work was, in the words of one member, "fraught with struggles" as they wrestled with challenging decisions about matters of personnel and the future direction of the school. Discussions ran to great length; meetings, held after school on Thursdays, generally lasted several hours. A core of members "steeped in anthroposophy" steered spirited debates of many, often diverse opinions and depth of philosophical thought.

Throughout these years, the College felt the imprint of a number of forceful personalities and leaders with strongly held opinions and, at times, heated interactions. Recalling these times, one member stated: "You had the sense that karmic streams had brought us together and karmic struggles were being worked out." Despite the obvious workload and responsibility, the College remained large and vibrant, and these years evoke warm memories in members who were active during that time. There was a sense of vital work being done, work that had direct impact on the course of the growing school. College work was perceived to be essential to the life of the school.

Crisis – and Opportunity

By the mid 1990s, over twenty-five years into the College's life, the mood had begun to shift and there were increasing signs of stress. Many of the founding leaders had by now left the school. The climate of strong personality was at times overwhelming; clashes led to wounded feelings and, on occasion, individuals walking out of meetings or even threatening to resign. Discord in the College mirrored general unease in the school. Demographics had begun to shift as a result of decisions to raise tuition at the end of the 1980s. Most of the founding families had by now graduated from the school. There was significant dissension regarding the future direction and identity of the school. This showed itself in actual splintering—in separate and competing parent organizations, in factions on the Board, and in the College (for a short period of time a small group met on weekends as an "alternative" College to discuss their opinions on the school's current condition and future course).

Within the College, administrative duties and personnel issues were becoming a significant burden, requiring large amounts of time and consistently derailing the group's attempts to deepen its work. One member recalled that they would optimistically commence the year with a plan of study, only to have that plan sidelined some time in October by a looming crisis, often concerning an issue of personnel. As a result, the College seemed increasingly divorced from the faculty at large. The College Chair had become a lightning rod for a range of community concerns, and College members were experiencing burnout. Increasingly, small groups of College members and non-College members gathered independently to discuss their concerns and to ponder solutions.

As a new millennium approached, it became increasingly apparent that the existing structure was no longer serving the school and that significant changes were needed. The College of Teachers had shrunk to a very small size; the handful of members who remained felt beleaguered, yet stayed on out of a sense of duty to the school and a desire to maintain the etheric space of the College, doing their best to keep alive a flame that had by now dwindled to a small flicker. The "them versus us" dynamic, powerful throughout the mid to late 1990s, had somewhat diminished; yet its replacement was hardly encouraging. To many members of the faculty, the small College simply appeared to be irrelevant to their concerns and work. A particularly bitter personnel issue divided the community, sapped strength, eroded parent trust, stretched relationships with the Board, and generally left people exhausted. Searching for next steps, the school did what many schools do in such circumstances: They called for help in the form of an outside consultant to clarify the situation and suggest a new direction.

Torin Finser, at that time head of the Waldorf teacher education program at Antioch University New England, was asked by the school to assess its governance and recommend changes. His first visit in June 2000 was preceded by a considerable amount of preparatory work by members of the College, faculty, and Board. His initial report described an unhappy situation of fractured leadership, "them versus us" dynamics, overlapping and inefficient responsibilities, cumbersome decision-making, and a high level of general frustration. Individuals acknowledged doing things "outside the system," and action often arose from personalities rather than policies. Additionally, he found concerns about inadequate teacher evaluation, a lack of consistent professional development, and an unclear and inadequate administrative structure. In this climate, leadership could not flourish; potential leaders were elevated, only to be chopped down. The school lacked a strong sense of a whole, focusing instead on meeting the day-to-day needs of separate sections of the school rather than building a collective future.

One of the gifts a consultant offers is the ability to reflect what an institution may already intuit or know, but in a form and with an objectivity that allow the message to be heard, understood, and accepted. This was our experience: There was little in this initial assessment that was truly surprising or unknown, yet there was much that had either never been stated or had been spoken only outside of meetings or in private conversations. Reassuringly, the report also noted that, despite the many serious concerns, there was much in the life of the school that appeared vibrant, healthy, and successful—especially as regards to work with the children and the curriculum. The crisis of leadership and governance had not yet filtered into the primary work of the school, but without intervention, this would probably have been only a matter of time. Through each finding and recommendation sounded the theme that the school's governance and leadership structure had run its course and was no longer capable of meeting the needs of the school as it entered the 21st century. Laid out starkly in black and white, this conclusion was now inescapable. A different type of action was required of us.

We agreed that we would need the ongoing help and support of an outside, objective party. Torin agreed to continue working with us but emphasized that any process of restructuring should be "highly participatory" and collaborative in the early stages to restore confidence in leadership and process. Several months of work by all faculty members, guided by Torin and in full consultation with the Board, led to a number of decisions, including a renewed commitment to the principle of a College of Teachers as an essential core of the school. In order to support this commitment, we recognized that a revitalized College would need structural and practical support. This support was initially focused in three major areas:

- Issues of personnel were identified as a major obstacle to the College's primary work and a factor that had led to alienation and division; therefore we would form an Executive Committee mandated to handle these matters.
- These issues often arose because of a lack of timely or effective evaluations and from inadequate professional development or training; we would form a Teacher Development Committee to meet these needs, providing early intervention and thereby reducing the possibility of crisis.
- A stronger and more empowered administrator would be needed to provide essential support to the College and to these two new committees; the role of administrator was redefined, a new job description crafted, and a search begun.

Re-founding

By June of 2001, we had worked through this new structure thoroughly in the full faculty circle and in smaller groups including Board members, College members, and faculty representatives. Through this process, the proposed structure had gained support and consensus. Preliminary mandate statements for the committees and for the College itself were crafted and agreed upon. These mandates spelled out the membership of each group, major tasks, and meeting structures. There was general acknowledgment that further refinement would be required once the groups were up and running. I was appointed as new administrator and began work that month with a revised and expanded job description. Even with these changes, we agreed that, if the renewed vision of the College of Teachers was to be realized, a radical step would be required to change the habits, patterns, history, and expectations associated with it. After consultation with the full faculty, with several former teachers and College members, and with current and past members of the Board, the existing College members decided, with some trepidation, that the College of Teachers as it had existed for over thirty years should disband and that a new College should be founded in its place.

Once we had made and agreed to this decision, a small group took on planning for the transition from one College to another. We continued this work over the summer months and addressed many questions, including how to

- provide a clear, evident separation from old forms to new ones
- best honor and provide continuity in our relationship with the Being of the school
- go about building confidence in the faculty and school community that this was, in fact, a new endeavor, not simply a continuation of business as usual

Given that concern, should the new body even be called a College of Teachers? Was there another, more appropriate name that would clearly signal a fresh start?

A number of decisions resulted from this questioning. We would indeed continue with the title "College of Teachers;" to us, this signified an alignment with the principle of pedagogical leadership, a reaffirmation of the commitment made back in 1965 that the faculty would be charged with responsibility for pedagogical and spiritual matters, and an endorsement of the years of dedicated collegial work that formed so much of the history of the school. We determined that we would respectfully and formally close the old College and allow a short pause before re-founding. Ultimately this pause would prove to be for only one night: We all sensed that we were at a vulnerable point in the school's biography, and we wanted the Hierarchies to see concrete evidence that we were sincere in our striving and intent and that we wished to rekindle a stronger relationship with the Being of our School.

We informed former College members, the leaders of The Association of Waldorf Schools of North America (AWSNA), and members of the Pedagogical Section Council of the school's decision. We were very conscious of the rich history of the College and of the colleagues who had carried its work on behalf of the school. In late August, a week before the school year was to start, the few remaining active members of the "old" College gathered in the school's garden just before sunset and proceeded to the bluffs overlooking the American River. There, we each voiced gratitude for the extraordinary contributions of all College members who had preceded us and for the source and foundation of our work, Rudolf Steiner. We voiced our hopes for the new group and for the future of the school. We read a verse and planted rosemary as a symbol of remembrance, then quietly dispersed, but that night it was hard to sleep. There was a sense of keeping vigil and an anxiety and vulnerability as we waited for the next day and the re-establishment of this core body.

The next morning, the entire faculty and staff gathered, along with invited guests including former faculty members, a representative of the Pedagogical Section Council, and representatives of AWSNA. Together, we entered a space that had been prepared for a simple ceremony and formed one large circle. There was an air of expectancy and subdued excitement;

this was a new venture and no one quite knew how it would unfold. After a reading of Rudolf Steiner's words to the faculty of the founding school and recitation of a verse, those faculty and staff who had reflected on the mandate and membership of the new College and felt drawn to serve as members of this new group stepped forward and signaled their intent by lighting a small taper from a central candle. A small circle of light slowly formed, held by the surrounding larger circle of colleagues and guests. It was a thrilling experience to step forward, to witness the membership of the group forming, and to feel the support of the larger circle of colleagues. We concluded with a song of celebration. A new College was born!

Becoming Established

The first meeting of the re-founded College was held just over a week later on Wednesday evening, September 5, 2001, when members gathered to read the College Imagination and begin our work. We had made a number of practical decisions to support this new group and to shift the habit life around the College. We shifted the meeting time to Wednesday evenings rather than the traditional time of after school on Thursdays. Initially, we made sure to keep Wednesday evenings free of any other meetings or school events. The resulting stillness of the campus lent a mood of focus and quiet concentration. The evening schedule made for a long day (we hold meetings of the full faculty after school on Wednesdays), but members agreed that its benefits outweighed the disadvantages. During the first months, colleagues who had not joined the College provided dinner before meetings as a wonderful gesture of support.

Initially, we focused on developing a better understanding of our mandate. Without the imperatives of business and administration, what would "responsible for the pedagogical and spiritual health of the school" through pedagogical and spiritual study actually look like? At first our work focused on establishing a structure for meetings and infrastructure for the school, with oversight of the formation of the two key support committees. We debated decision-making and agreed to adopt a consensus model within the College. We explored meeting format, selected a facilitator and agenda-setter, and created a third position, a "navigator," whose task was to witness the work of the College and to warn us when, as we agreed was likely, it was veering back into old territory of personnel issues and school management. We decided that the new group would not have an individual leader; the position of College Chair was no more. We made this decision because the position had become highly charged and vulnerable to community frustration or upset. It was no longer a position that anyone would step into willingly. In its place, we attempted collaborative leadership by appointing agenda-setter, facilitator, and navigator. The greatest challenge to this model proved to be the practical task of finding a time during the week for the group to meet and plan. Many tasks that previously lived with the College Chair fell to me as administrator; this transition was facilitated by the fact that I was a College member and former class teacher. We appointed College members to key committees to help strengthen relationships and ensure direct communication.

As we found our way in those early months, we focused on artistic explorations of the Opening and Closing Verses and the College Imagination, which were variously expressed through sketching, modeling, movement, eurythmy, and writing. We attempted to employ the principles of Goethean conversation in our treatment of a range of topics that, over the course of the first year, included exploration of a nursery program, study of the developmental stages of adolescence and the high school curriculum, questions of stewardship of our campus, and— perhaps inevitably for a College that came to form on the eve of the events of 9/11—robust discussions about nationalism, globalism, the place of a flag on campus, and the nature of our times. These discussions led to our selecting Rudolf Steiner's *Manifestations of Karma* as our first formal study.

Evolution and Change

Creating new structures and forms did not automatically result in new behaviors. Institutional habit life is strong and runs deep, and it took some time to refine and communicate the new format and new expectations. Recognizing that the school was still in transition, we continued our work towards a renewal of governance through an administrative audit, conducted in 2002 by John Bloom and the Rudolf Steiner Foundation. The audit report summarized conditions at that time, a year after the re-founding of the College: "There is a longing for a kind of renewal in the administrative life that would parallel the renewal experienced by those members of the faculty who chose to reform the College of Teachers." It went on to note the success of the re-founding: "There is an important model in this renewal in that an old, "ineffectual" form had to pass away to allow a new form to emerge. …The theme of renewal or rediscovery of purpose in the College of Teachers, and the positive effect it has had upon the pedagogical life of the school, surfaced in several conversations."[5] Through the audit we began a process of clarifying and strengthening the administration, under its new leadership, to better support the work of the school.

The College continued to clarify its function and form. Evening meetings proved to be a deterrent to some prospective members, precluding their participation. It did allow those involved in the athletic program to participate (there were no practices or games on Wednesdays), but during the first few years, only one colleague took advantage of this possibility.

Over time, the sanctity of Wednesday evenings as College-only nights was eroded by the busy life of a K–12 school with competing calendar needs and constant demands for space and time. As a result, the quiet mood on campus dissipated and, at times, College attendance was compromised as members juggled competing demands.

Initially, members made one-year commitments to the group. Unlike the old model, in which there would be a conversation and invitation, colleagues were free to consider the conditions of membership and to decide whether to join. Without the filter of an invitation or conversation process, two founding members quickly discovered that the experience was not what they had expected and resigned rather unhappily from the group. Neither of them had prior College experience and both appeared to be overwhelmed or disappointed by the reality of the new mandate. Otherwise, resignations of College members have, in fact, been rare in the ten years since re-founding.

The formation of mandated committees afforded the College the freedom to take up its work of active research and study. However, it took some years to refine and clarify the roles of these committees; in fact, this remains an ongoing process as the school evolves. In the early years there was a lot of sorting out of what belonged where. The College retained oversight of faculty hiring and student acceptances. It continued to give input into the budget process as it affected program and personnel.

Communication proved to be the greatest challenge to all parties as we attempted to find a balance between ensuring the College was sufficiently informed to be able to make decisions while avoiding replicating the work of mandated groups. Personnel matters continued to present the most complex challenges: what to do when the Steering Committee was confronted with concerns about a member of the College and how to inform the College in a timely and appropriate way of a sensitive personnel issue without re-creating the work and triggering the very concerns about privacy and confidentiality that had in part motivated delegation in the first place.

The building and maintaining of trust was also an ongoing challenge—trust between the new Steering Committee and the College, between the College and the faculty, and between the Steering Committee and the faculty at large. Relationships tended to become strained whenever the Steering Committee was addressing performance issues with a colleague, and the always-difficult decision to let a colleague go inevitably caused ripples and upset and raised questions about the process, fairness, and work of the Steering Committee. The old "them versus us" dynamic was easily awakened, provoked by the imperative for confidentiality around personnel issues that quickly gave rise to concerns of secrecy, exclusivity, or undue power.

These concerns were mitigated to some extent by the nature of Steering Committee membership: three positions were linked to roles (Administrator, High School Coordinator, and Lower School Coordinator) and two positions were revolving (representative of the College of Teachers and pedagogical representative of the faculty at large). As a result, over a number of years several teachers have shared the weight and responsibility of the Steering Committee's work, thereby helping to build trust and support and to mitigate old patterns of mistrust and divisiveness.

It took a long time to shift community perceptions and expectations; there were many years of habit around what the College was supposed to do and what it was responsible for. The Board and community continued to direct questions to the College that more properly belonged to the Steering Committee and, at least during the first years, they continued to hanker after a College Chair. As a result, they would feel frustration and anxiety that things were falling through the cracks—as, from time to time, they inevitably did.

Current Form

Our College model has shifted and evolved in the ten-plus years since its re-founding, and it will no doubt continue to need refinement in response to the ever-changing life and needs of the school. Its present iteration can be summarized quite briefly. The College of Teachers continues to be regarded as an essential organ of the school, with overarching responsibility for its spiritual and pedagogical health—a phrase that is relatively easy to utter, but complicated to enact.

The College meets every week but takes a break during the summer months; this year we changed our meeting time from Wednesday evening back to the more traditional Thursday afternoon to open up the possibility for new membership. It is currently thirteen members strong; smaller than the lively Colleges of the 1980s and 90s, much larger than the College of the late 1990s, and the largest it has been for several years of its re-founded life. These thirteen members represent less than thirty percent of the potential pool of eligible faculty and staff. All sections of the school—Kindergarten, Lower School, High School—as well as Administration are represented in the current group. Oddly, the current membership of thirteen has eleven women and two men, the exact opposite configuration of our current Board. It has not traditionally been so gender unbalanced.

We hold an annual re-dedication ceremony prior to which the mandate and membership conditions are reviewed within the College and with the wider faculty circle. During the re-dedication ceremony, colleagues are invited to step onto or off the College. For the first few years we held this ceremony in the spring; more recently, we have conducted a review in June and held our re-dedication in late August as part of our back-to-school work. The ceremony is very similar in form to the one that marked the re-founding. This year, we asked members for a two-year commitment to help build greater continuity; previously we had set a minimum of one year. Although we have conditions for membership, the decision to join remains a free, individual deed. College members may encourage colleagues to join, but there is no formal invitation issued. It is not considered to be part of a member's teaching or administrative load. Occasionally this process does not work, but most members remain as active College participants for several years. Two current members have been on the College continuously since its re-founding; both were members of the "old" College (I am one of those individuals). One colleague recently rejoined the College; she had previously served in the mid 1990s.

Membership is open to any member of the faculty or staff who has worked at the school for at least one year (now revised to two) and feels sufficiently familiar with the school. The considerations for membership have remained largely unchanged since the re-founding. They include:

- What is my relationship to anthroposophy? Anthroposophy provides the guiding star for College work.
- How will a commitment to the College affect my current work in the school?
- Is my family or personal life supportive of this additional commitment?
- Am I building and maintaining healthy relationships with my colleagues? Am I in good standing in my professional life?

- Am I committed to the school for the foreseeable future; am I able to make a commitment for a period of one year (or more) with regular attendance and any necessary preparation?

The College has been fairly successful in holding to its commitment to study and research, and work has deepened over time. We strive to connect the themes of our study to phenomena of the school. For example, last year our study was focused on the Eightfold Path, with texts drawn from Rudolf Steiner, Georg Kühlewind, and the Buddha. We attempted to apply our insights to different aspects of the life of the school and to bring the fruits of our study to full faculty meetings. This year we have returned to basics: taking up the study of Steiner's *How to Know Higher Worlds*, striving to build dialogue around our individual inner work, and refining our capacities for observation and sensing of the school. We have become more disciplined about identifying work that is not ours and sending it where it belongs, especially in any crisis or emergency situation. As administrator, and the only person in the school required to serve on the College, I attempt to provide considerable support through agenda and calendar setting, provision of data, and the implementation of policies and decisions.

To begin, we scheduled meetings to last two hours; more recently we have shortened them to ninety minutes. A typical agenda begins with the College Imagination and Opening Verse, followed by a period of approximately thirty minutes for discussion and reflection on our current "spiritual" study (such as the Eightfold Path or *How to Know Higher Worlds*). We then usually turn our attention for approximately thirty or forty minutes to our current pedagogical study (currently an examination of what is essential in a Waldorf school), leaving a brief time at the end for reports and announcements. We attempt to link our "spiritual" and "pedagogical" studies. Meetings conclude with the Closing Verse. Occasionally we require additional time, but this is rare.

The Teacher Development Committee originally had responsibility for both faculty development and evaluation. We recognized that these tasks could potentially stand in conflict, so evaluation was moved to the Steering Committee (originally named the Executive Committee, but renamed after several years to avoid confusion with the Board Executive Committee). Membership of the Teacher Development Committee includes a representative from the Kindergarten, the Lower School, the High School, and the College of Teachers. Initially, the full faculty nominated these representatives, but we soon realized that ownership and appointment by each separate section strengthened communication and support for the work. The Teacher Development Committee currently oversees mentoring, the creation of individual professional development plans and goals, and the planning and execution of in-service days. Several years ago, recognizing that faculty expectations and needs were changing and that different types of agreements were called for, we instituted minimum requirements for professional development hours. The Teacher Development Committee monitors completion of those hours, providing suggestions and support as needed.

The Steering Committee oversees faculty hiring and evaluation. It addresses school needs, performance issues, and a wide range of other concerns. Its mandate specifies that it handle crises and "issues that are not taken care of by any other group"—a category that can be a catch-all for a wide range of topics. The work of the Steering Committee can be weighty and challenging at times, but we have found advantages to having a small, more specialized group addressing these aspects of our work. This frees up the larger circle, and skills can be honed and essential knowledge built. Confidentiality is less challenging with the smaller group. Because of these factors, when the group is working harmoniously it can be tempting to fix membership into place and extend the terms of the College and faculty representatives rather than providing for the rotation of membership. The model requires trust and communication— not always easy to achieve or maintain, but meriting ongoing awareness and effort. A strong administration is needed to support this model; the administrator role as currently defined almost certainly requires someone with a teaching background and considerable knowledge of Waldorf pedagogy.

We have continued to differentiate and delegate. Our high school has over 150 students, and several years ago we recognized the fundamentally different, more complex nature of a high school's organization and the need for greater autonomy and nimbleness in its operation. This led to the formation of a High School Coordinating Committee, overseen by the Steering Committee and mandated to have significant independence in administering the high school. The High School Coordinating Committee, chaired by the High School Coordinator, is comprised of department heads and the athletic director. This has resulted in a much more harmonious and efficient high school, yet has recently led us to examine what it means to have and to maintain a K–12 program and how to protect and further develop this important aspect of our school's identity.

There has been gradual and ongoing redefinition of the scope of the College's responsibilities. We slowly learned that mandating really did mean clarifying, handing over, letting go, and trusting. That was not an easy lesson for a group of teachers accustomed to being in command. Although the College retains ultimate responsibility for the direction of the school, on many issues such as student acceptances, and even in some instances the hiring of colleagues, it is consulted and informed but does not engage directly in the work. Currently, very few decisions take place within the College. We have much greater separation between the "spirit" and the "real practical life" than in former times. The ongoing challenge is to maintain connection and communication, to truly remember that "Spirit is never without matter, matter never without Spirit"[6] and to practice accordingly. In a Waldorf school, although business must be conducted in a business-like manner, if we are to achieve success it can never be disconnected from the impulse that stands behind our work or from relationship to the school's Being and mission. This statement is a given in the pedagogical aspects of our work but is more easily forgotten or neglected when we turn to business and management.

Current and Future Challenges and Opportunities

Communication remains perhaps our greatest ongoing challenge. The primary work of the College is not easy to report on; it is experiential, at times intensely personal, and often there is no "product" to present. Concerns about confidentiality have also had an impact and were one of our original reasons for removing personnel issues from consideration by the full College. We live in an age of requirements for compliance, increasingly complex regulations, and the potential of significant institutional consequences for ignorance or impropriety.

As noted earlier, relationships have been most strained when the Steering Committee has confronted serious concerns about a colleague's performance. In a horizontal, consensus-based structure, it is asking a great deal to empower a small group to deal with questions of a colleague's future—and to be unable to communicate in detail about it. We have struggled with appropriate formats for reporting to the faculty, the Board, and the community, yet we know that without clear and regular reporting, trust can quickly erode.

On a positive note, it is interesting that we have weathered the past few years of recession and resulting economic and enrollment pressures with remarkably high morale; one might dare to hope that this is to some extent the result of the somewhat invisible work of the College. We see much less strain among College members and less illness, compared to those troubled days of the late 1990s. A single teacher no longer bears the weight of College Chair duties. Although much of this work now resides with me as administrator, it is compatible with my other responsibilities and duties, and I have found that my membership on the College has continued to provide a source of strength, learning, and centering.

College meetings lack the drama of former times. A College member with long experience of meetings noted that the mood is generally much more harmonious—and much less intense. She felt that this is in part a reflection of the redefined work of the College; with many potentially contentious issues and decisions removed, the possibility of conflict has been significantly reduced. Comparing present to former times, she also noted that there seems to be less struggling of several, at times competing, leaders. The mood is more horizontal and less charged.

At various times, including the current year, we have opened portions of College meetings to any member of the faculty and staff who wishes to attend. Few have taken advantage of this invitation; it can be difficult to step in and out of an ongoing group, yet the gesture of inclusion is important. It remains a challenge to maintain a climate of "us" and avoid fragmentation into parts. This is a school with a long history of division into kindergarten, lower school, and high school faculties. The three groups come together only once each month for a shared meeting. "Them and us" dynamics and competing needs surface easily—between sections of the faculty, College and faculty, and Steering Committee and faculty or College. Knowing that this is a repeating motif in the school's biography, we need to constantly strive to build in shared work, transparency, and regular reporting. It is very easy to forget this in the busy-ness of a school year. Our K–12 identity is a shared value, one that affords many opportunities, and we are currently looking at ways of strengthening cross-school ties and collaboration within the faculty and with other bodies within the school.

The tendency towards "them and us" is but one of a number of our recurring challenges. In any institution, it is important to note the conditions of birth and early years and the themes that resound throughout the years. Anthroposophy was not strongly articulated in the founding impulse of this school. It was brought to the forefront by the "Kimberton Five" and soon found its home in the College of Teachers. It has been the source of College work ever since. It is interesting to note that the Five had two conditions: They would be granted authority over all pedagogical matters and the Board would relieve the school of a burden of debt. This can easily be interpreted as an early separation of spirit (the realm of the College) and matter (the realm of the Board).

Recently, the College has begun to re-examine the wisdom of this separation and its role in the wider governance of the school. It is likely that this will be a focus of significant work for the next phase of the school's development. Joint College-Board work has been intermittent since the collaboration that led to the College re-founding and administrative restructuring and the completion of a major building project in 2007. Both groups have relied increasingly on the administrator as a primary point of contact, intersection, and—at times—

interpretation, rather than engaging in the challenge of more direct contact.

Without the intensity of a major joint project, distance between the Board and College has become evident. In 2008, after examining the effectiveness and intent of College/faculty representation on the Board, the College decided to reduce its presence on the Board from three to two members and to no longer have a College representative serve as vice president of the Board. Since then the College has manifested a degree of indifference towards the Board. Without regular, direct communication, it can become easy for "spirit" to disregard the importance of "matter" and for "matter" to disregard the significance of "spirit."

The effects of distance are showing, and as we set the school's course for the next five to ten years—a recurring task that is necessary in order to navigate safely and with integrity through new terrain of a changed economy and a new generation of parents and teachers—several old, familiar questions are back before us. What does it mean in practice to have responsibility for the spiritual and pedagogical life of the school? What is the role of anthroposophy in the life of this school? How can the College effectively and helpfully share its work with the Board? How is anthroposophy to be represented at the Board table? How can both groups work collaboratively to shape a shared vision for the school that will protect and nurture the very essence of our work? How can we balance essential business matters—the need for economy, efficiency, and legality of operations—with the intangible yet essential aspects of our work? What happens if these two vital aspects of the school—spirit and matter—become disconnected? Important work to address these questions is underway with dialogue currently taking place between the College Steering Committee and the Board Executive Committee.

The Sacramento Waldorf School stands on the banks of a large river; change and motion are recurring themes of its biography. The model of a College described above, with significant separation of spirit and practical, has carried us forward for over ten years. The model continues to change and self-correct in response to the evolving needs of the school. Although it calls for significant separation of spirit and practical, the two remain continuously linked within the pedagogical life of the school by common principles, language, and understanding and by a structure that ensures shared membership of groups to maintain communication and trust. As we enter a new phase of examining relationships among College, Board, and administration, we are likely to need further refinement of our model and to be open to change. Through this work it will be the responsibility of the College "to say to [y]ourselves: We will do everything material in the light of the Spirit and we will seek the light of the Spirit in such a way that it ignites in us a warmth for our practical deeds"[7] Both are essential for the future health of our school, and we need to find new ways of allowing these poles to infuse one another. Through this new phase of our work, it is likely that a commitment to the central importance of a College of Teachers, and its role in guarding and guiding the mission of the school, will remain as a vital core and source of strength for the school.

Endnotes

1. Rudolf Steiner, *Supersensible Knowledge and Social-Pedagogical Life-Force* (Stuttgart, 1919).
2. *Education as an Art*, The Rudolf Steiner School Association, Vol. 21, 1961, p. 14.
3. Historical records and personal correspondence courtesy of Betty Staley.
4. Sacramento Waldorf Schools Bylaws, 1970.

5. Sacramento Waldorf School Administration Audit Report, Rudolf Steiner Foundation, June, 2002.
6. Op. cit., Steiner.
7. Ibid.

Core Principles of Waldorf Education

Pedagogical Section Council of North America
(January 2013)

Waldorf education can be characterized as having seven core principles. Each one of them can be the subject of a lifelong study. Nevertheless, they can be summarized in the following manner:

Image of the Human Being: The human being in its essence is a being of Spirit, soul, and body. Childhood and adolescence, from birth to age 21, are the periods during which the Spirit-soul gradually takes hold of the physical instrument that is our body. The Self is the irreducible spiritual individuality within each one of us, which continues its human journey through successive incarnations.

Phases of Child Development: This process of embodiment has an archetypal sequence of approximately seven-year phases, and each child's development is an individual expression of the archetype. Each phase has unique and characteristic physical, emotional and cognitive dimensions.

Developmental Curriculum: The curriculum is created to meet and support the phase of development of the individual and the class. From birth to age 7 the guiding principle is that of imitation; from 7 to 14 the guiding principle is that of following the teacher's guidance; during the high school years the guiding principles are idealism and the development of independent judgment.

Freedom in Teaching: Rudolf Steiner gave curriculum indications with the expectation that "the teacher should invent the curriculum at every moment." Out of the understanding of child development and Waldorf pedagogy, the Waldorf teacher is expected to meet the needs of the children in the class out of his/her insights and the circumstances of the school. Interferences with the freedom of the teacher by the school, parents, standardized testing regimen, or the government, while they may be necessary in a specific circumstance (for safety or legal reasons, for example), are nonetheless compromises.[1]

Methodology of Teaching: there are a few key methodological guidelines for the grade school and high school teachers. Early Childhood teachers work with these principles appropriate to the way in which the child before the age of 7 learns, out of imitation rather than direct instruction:

- Artistic metamorphosis: The teacher should understand, internalize, and then present the topic in an artistic form.[2]
- From experience to concept: The direction of the learning process should proceed from the students' soul activities of willing, through feeling to thinking. In the high school the context of the experience is provided at the outset.[3]
- Holistic process: proceeding from the whole to the parts and back again, and addressing the whole human being.
- Use of rhythm and repetition.[4]

Relationships: The task of the teacher is to work with the developing individuality of each student and with the class as a whole. Truly pedagogical human relationships cannot be replaced by instructions utilizing computers or other electronic means; human encounter is essential and irreplaceable. Healthy working relationships with parents and colleagues are also essential to the wellbeing of the class community and the school.

Spiritual Orientation: In order to cultivate the imaginations, inspirations, and intuitions needed for their work, Rudolf Steiner gave the teachers an abundance of guidance for developing an inner, meditative life. This guidance includes individual, professional meditations and an imagination of the circle of teachers forming an organ of spiritual perception. Faculty and individual study, artistic activity, and research form additional facets of ongoing professional development.

Endnotes

1. A note about school governance: While not directly a pedagogical matter, school governance can be an essential aspect of freedom in teaching. Just as a developmental curriculum should support the phases of child development, school governance should support the teachers' pedagogical freedom (while maintaining the school's responsibilities towards society).
2. The term "artistic" does not necessarily mean the traditional arts (singing, drawing, sculpting, etc.), but rather that, like those arts, the perceptually manifest reveals something invisible through utilizing perceptible media. Thus a math problem or science project can be just as artistic as storytelling or painting.
3. This mirrors the development of human cognition, which is at first active in the limbs and only later in the head.
4. There are four basic rhythms with which the Waldorf teacher works. The most basic of those is the day-night (or two-day)

rhythm. Material that is presented on a given day is allowed to "go to sleep" before it is reviewed and brought to conceptual clarity on the following day. A second rhythm is that of the week. It is "the interest rhythm" and teachers strive to complete an engagement with a topic within a week of working on it. A paper that is returned to the student after more than a week will no longer be interesting to the student. The only interesting thing will be the teacher's comments, but the topic itself is already past the "interest window." A third rhythm is that of four weeks. A block, or unit of instruction, is usually best covered in a four-week period. This life-rhythm can be understood in contemplation of feminine reproductive cycles, for example, and can be said to bring a topic to a temporary level of maturity. The last of the pedagogical rhythms is that of a year. This is the time it can take for a new concept to be mastered to the degree that it can be used as a capacity. Thus a mathematical concept introduced early in third grade should be mastered sufficiently to be assumed as a capacity for work at the beginning of fourth grade.

Contributors

Liz Beaven has been the administrator of the Sacramento Waldorf School since 2001. Prior to that, she was a class teacher for thirteen years. She is a delegate for AWSNA and a DANA representative. Her interests include school governance and organization, student experience, and questions related to Waldorf education in the modern world.

Holly Koteen-Soulé has been an early childhood teacher since 1988, working at the Seattle Waldorf School and (as a founding teacher) at the Bright Water School, Seattle. She is a core faculty member and Director of Early Childhood Teacher Education of Sound Circle Center in Seattle and a member of the Pedagogical Section Council.

Elan Leibner is the editor of the *Research Bulletin*, a member of the Pedagogical Section Council, and a freelance mentor and consultant to schools. He was a class teacher at the Waldorf School of Princeton for eighteen years. Since 2008 he has been involved in adult education, consulting, and mentoring in Waldorf schools in the U.S., U.K., and (soon) China.

Betty Staley has been involved in Waldorf education for over fifty years. She has taught grade school, high school, and college classes and was one of the founders of Rudolf Steiner College in Fair Oaks, CA. She is the Director of the Waldorf

High School Teacher Education Program at RSC, a member of the Pedagogical Section Council, a member of the Board of the Alliance for Public Waldorf Education, and an author of numerous books.

Roberto Trostli has been active in Waldorf education as a class teacher, high school teacher, adult educator, and lecturer for thirty years. He is the author of *Physics Is Fun: a Sourcebook for Teachers*, numerous articles on Waldorf education, and a dozen plays for children. He edited and introduced *Rhythms of Learning and Teaching Language Arts in the Waldorf School*. Roberto currently teaches at the Richmond Waldorf School, VA.

Jane Wulsin has been a class teacher at Green Meadow Waldorf School since 1979, taking four classes through grades 1–8. For many years she was a member of the Pedagogical Section Council and AWSNA. She has been active over the years in mentoring and in adult education, and she is currently teaching the fourth grade.

Haiku 1
Ursula Stone

oil on canvas
three panels, 10" x 10"

Silky water falls

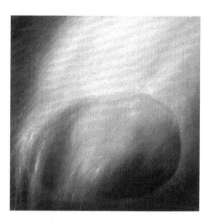

Over moss encrusted rock

Elemental art